WE SURVIVED

WE SURVIVED

A Mother's Story of Japanese Captivity

Nell van de Graaff

with drawings by the author

CHIVERS

British Library Cataloguing in Publication Data available

This Large Print edition published by BBC Audiobooks Ltd, Bath, 2006.
Published by arrangement with the author

U.K. Hardcover ISBN 1 4056 3723 4
            ISBN 13: 978 1 405 63723 7
U.K. Softcover ISBN 1 4056 3724 2
            ISBN 13: 978 1 405 63724-4

Printed and bound in Great Britain by
Antony Rowe Ltd., Chippenham, Wiltshire

INTRODUCTION

Encouraged by my children, I decided to record my wartime experiences in Indonesia. I let my thoughts drift back to those grim years from 1942 to 1945 and my imprisonment by the Japanese. When they invaded Indonesia in 1942 I lived on the island of Java. My husband, an officer in the Netherlands East Indies Army, was taken prisoner and, with thousands of fellow soldiers, transported to Singapore and later Burma.

I fled from Central Java with our three young children prior to the invasion and on my husband's advice went to West Java, which he felt was a safer place to be at that time. It was there in the mountains in a little stone cottage surrounded by terraced ricefields that I heard the announcement of the unconditional surrender by the Dutch government.

This was the beginning of a dark, insecure, terrifying period, relieved only by the generosity and compassion of the two Indonesian brothers from whom I rented the cottage. They and a friend of theirs hid us from marauding Japanese storm troops, protected us and shared their meagre food supply with us. My three children were aged four and a half, three, and one year, and I was twenty-six and expecting my fourth baby. She was born in

1

June 1942 in a small mission hospital. About four months later we were all rounded up by the Japanese and with hundreds of Dutch women and children from that area were taken to a prison camp in Bandung.

We were kept there about two years, during which time conditions deteriorated badly, contagious illnesses raged out of control and starvation claimed many lives.

After our term in the Bandung prison camp we were transferred to the notorious Tjideng camp in Jakarata, which proved for many to be the straw that broke the camel's back. Children, especially, died there in large numbers. About six months later I was sent with my children to a newly established hospital camp just outside Jakarta. Our small group—only a few young children were included—formed the nursing staff and workers who cared for the terminally ill prisoners brought in from the several camps in and around Jakarta. We were liberated from the Japanese on 15 August 1945. I knew that if the war had lasted another two months my children and I would not have survived. It was a miracle that we made it to celebrate this long-awaited freedom and the reunion with my husband, their father, in the following December.

I have never forgotten the care and devotion of our three Indonesian friends before our imprisonment and in 1971 I decided to return to Indonesia to try to find them. The last few chapters are devoted to this pilgrimage, but the main part of the story concerns the three prison camps, the suffering of the imprisoned women and children, their will to survive, and their indomitable spirits. How adaptable the human spirit is in times of adversity—it seems to shine like a light in the dark, like a beacon of hope.

This photograph was taken at Christmas 1950 a few months before the family emigrated to Australia in April 1951.

From left to right:
John (37), Albert (4), Johnny (13), Manya (11), Nell (35), Peter (9), Nelleke (8).
Nell is expecting a sixth child, Bill, who was born in Australia in June 1951.

CHAPTER ONE

Evening had fallen swiftly, and with it came the familiar night sounds that rose from the terraced ricefields below. The shrill song of the cicadas drifted from the bamboo stools and hibiscus bushes surrounding the whitewashed cottage. I sat in the cane chair, gazing into the soft-golden flame of the oil lamp before me on the table. The tiny enclosed verandah shielded me like a cocoon and now and then I looked out through the windows into the darkness, where more and more little lights came on, flickering at first then shining with more confidence. They were the lamps in the small houses among the ricefields and also higher up the hillside along the road that wound through the village.

That morning I tore off the paper strips that had covered the windows for the last few months so that light could not be seen from outside. It had been a military order intended to prevent enemy planes from distinguishing targets at night. Now that we were given the all-clear our lives were supposed to function normally again. But what was normal? It was announced over the radio the same morning that the Dutch East Indies government had surrendered unconditionally to the Japanese invaders. The day was 8 March 1942. The village we were in was called Nagrok, in the hills above Sukabumi in West Java.

The Netherlands had surrendered to Germany in May 1940 after a few bloody days of intense fighting. The war in Europe then had seemed so far away from the thousands of Dutch residents in the Indonesian islands, but the distress and uncertainty about the fate of relatives and friends in the old country weighed heavily on us. Rapidly the situation in our part of the world then started to change. Singapore fell in February 1942 as the Japanese came surging southwards, unstoppable, it seemed. The Dutch Air Force dispatched all available aeroplanes and personnel from Indonesia to Singapore in an effort to halt the advance there. When the Japanese forces swiftly descended on Indonesia there was little the Dutch East Indies Army could do—the country had lost its entire air force during the battle over Singapore, thought to be unconquerable.

For the five months until February 1942, I lived in the Dutch military base of Magelang, near Jogja, in Central Java. My husband John was a professional officer, a military engineer, and we lived in a lovely home with our three children. Towards the end of February John came home from the barracks late one evening and told me that all army personnel were to leave Central Java and retreat to and around the city of Bandung in West Java in an attempt to make a last stand there. Being in charge of the Signal Corps, John would have to leave the next day with the complete Headquarters staff of Central Java. He did not want to leave me and the children behind and arranged for us to borrow a colleague's car (we were not so fortunate to have one ourselves) complete with driver and helpmate. Just before Headquarters departed from the city, he wanted me to take the children and also a good friend of ours and her little baby, and travel by car via Bandung to Sukabumi in West Java. We knew that my eldest brother Bill had been evacuated to Sukabumi the previous week from Billiton, a small island between Singapore and Java. The plan was to leave Central Java and reach the West as soon as possible, as invasion by the Japanese seemed imminent.

Two days later in the early morning we departed: the children, aged four, three and one year, and I, the two Indonesians, and my friend Georgette and her six-month-old baby. How do you say: Goodbye. When will we see each other again? or, Please, hold me, don't let me go! or Children, kiss Daddy goodbye? Was this really happening or was it a nightmare? And then the doors were shut and the car moved off—one last wave and we were out of sight.

We had with us a bag of rice, some canned food, drinks and a minimum of clothing. The children soon fell asleep, it was already very hot, the roads were dusty and the busy morning traffic slowed us down.

As I sat on the verandah remembering these events from a few weeks back, a sound interrupted my reverie. Manya, my three-year-old daughter, was stirring in her sleep and I heard her murmuring 'Daddy'. She rolled over to her brothers and snuggled up to them. I pulled up the thin blanket and covered them gently. They were now all fast asleep, my friend and her baby too, on the cotton mattresses that covered about a quarter of the single-roomed cottage. I held the oil lamp high so that I could see in all the corners to make sure everything was all right and that the mosquito coil was still burning. Returning to the verandah and the only chair we had—it was an old cane one—I listened in the lamplight to the chorus of the frogs in the ricefields.

I felt strangely at peace, really somewhat elated, in the relative safety of the small house, as if suspended above a world in turmoil, out of reach, out of harm. Settling back in the rickety chair, I let my thoughts wander again, my hands folded over my swollen belly, my fourth child. I thought once more of that morning when we left Magelang.

It was a full carload that drove off to the west through winding mountain roads and stretches of dusty highway. A feeling of foreboding made us feel uneasy, together with a constant awareness of danger; we were afraid of driving into an ambush, a possibility, as there had been reports of Japanese commandos parachuting in to secluded areas. In my bag was a revolver. It was given to me by a friend who knew I could handle it, as I once belonged to a rifle club and had won target shooting trophies. It gave me a feeling of protection, in case the worst came to the worst, but at the same time I doubted if I could ever bring myself to use it on a human target.

As the hours wore on and the sun beat down relentlessly from a brilliant blue sky, the heat became almost unbearable. The children were carsick, thirsty and tired, and we had finished our last bottle of water. At midday we arrived at Tjilatjap, a city on the south coast of Java, half-way to Bandung. I asked the driver to pull up at a large hotel and park in the shade of a large tree. We all tumbled out of the car, nauseous, dirty and crumpled, and made our way up the steps and into the big reception hall. The driver and his mate went off with some money I had given them to buy themselves cold drinks and a bowl of rice and vegetables at the foodstalls that lined the main street. It was just on lunch time at the hotel when we arrived and a servant with a deep-sounding gong was summoning the guests to the dining hall. We were an incongruous sight amid fashionably dressed ladies and gentlemen thinking only about what would be on the menu—a small group of tired, sickly looking refugees who made a beeline for the toilets and the washbasins.

Georgette, my friend, normally very prim and proper, flopped down on the sofa in the immaculate entrance hall with its chandeliers and silver ornaments, and without further ado unbuttoned her blouse and began feeding her baby, oblivious of the stares and whispers. When we told the receptionists where we had come from and what the situation was in Central Java, they were most surprised and appeared to think we were exaggerating. We drank and had something to eat, refilled all our water bottles, packed lots of sandwiches and some fruit, and then set off again.

During the late afternoon our pace slowed down. The mountain roads leading up to the plateau where Bandung was were very steep in places. Several strategic bridges were mined, we knew, and we had to cross them with great care.

Evening in the tropics comes unannounced—there is no twilight. When we entered Bandung just after 6 p.m., it was dark, with no lights shining through the blackened windows. In the sky was an array of searchlights, their beams crossing overhead, trying to detect enemy planes. At several spots our car was stopped, inspected briefly and then waved on.

After quite some searching—because with lights dimmed it was hard to find our way—we arrived at the home of relatives of mine, where my second eldest brother Jan, a civilian, and his wife and two young daughters were staying. We quickly refreshed ourselves and had something to eat, then looking each other in the eyes, we hugged each other aware of the imminent danger. We knew that the road to Sukabumi would be long and difficult with hardly any light to go by. My brother held me in his arms, then gently urged me to get into the car. I never saw him again—he died two years later in a Japanese prison camp.

Just outside Bandung we came upon a long convoy of tanks and armoured cars—English troops on their way to Jakarta to board British warships. For the last few months Allied troops had been stationed on Java but, realising that trying to defend these islands would be a hopeless cause, they evacuated swiftly and completely. The winding mountain roads were almost blocked by the slow army vehicles. Utterly exhausted, the children had fallen asleep, and I remember feeling safe being part of an armoured convoy. After a while our ways parted, the convoy went rumbling on towards Jakarta and we turned off on to the road for Sukabumi. It was absolutely quiet now, except for the eerie sound of an occasional high-flying plane—was it ours or the enemy's?

11

Sukabumi was a small town in the mountains and the road was steadily climbing by this stage. We had to stop a few times and ask directions and we found out by chance that the Hotel Salabintana, where my eldest brother Bill and his family (and other evacuees from the island of Billiton) were staying, was only half an hour past Sukabumi. Towards midnight we arrived at the old, sprawling hotel which was still a hive of activity, although the sounds were subdued and there were very few lights. As we had heard, the hotel and its extensive grounds and outhouses were being used as a receiving depot for evacuees from the outlying islands, in this case Sumatra, Banka and Billiton.

We collected our few belongings from the car, and I shook hands with our driver and his mate. I could scarcely find words to thank them enough for their kindness and their invaluable help and I praised their skill in manoeuvring us through the many dangerous situations. The least I could do was to give them a handsome reward and the next day, in the early morning, they returned to Central Java.

It took us about half an hour before we located my brother Bill, who with his wife and four children occupied one large room in the hotel. We also bedded down there on a few mattresses. Everyone collapsed, exhausted, except my brother and I, who sat together for several hours. He told me about his narrow escape when the ship he was aboard along with the last evacuees from Billiton was sunk by a Japanese bomber; only fifty or sixty survivors in lifeboats were picked up a few days later by two Dutch seaplanes. Luckily Bill's wife and children and the wives and children of the other employees of the Billiton Tin Company had been evacuated a few days earlier and were already installed at the hotel.

Early the next morning Georgette and I and the children had to leave the hotel, as it was already overcrowded with evacuees. The manager was able to secure us a place to stay in the nearby village of Nagrok, on the other side of a deep ravine from the hotel.

Minsha, a kind German woman who was married to a Dutch man, drove us to the little cottage which was owned by two Indonesian brothers, Atik and Tjètjè, who lived with their families in two simple dwellings a stone's throw away. For the past few years Minsha had been living in Nagrok, where she had a big house and some tiny bungalows for holiday letting. She showed us a lot of love and helped us in many ways. She had established a First Aid Office in Nagrok and had a special relationship with the villagers who held her in high esteem.

So there we were, settling down amongst the village people, sharing their anxiety and insecurity, staying quietly in our darkened homes at night, while during the day the children played with their young neighbours and with a big white goat and noisy, scrawny chickens. About ten days after we arrived the announcement came over the radio that the Dutch East Indies government had ceased to exist. It heralded a period of change, the like of which we could not have foreseen in our wildest imagination.

CHAPTER TWO

During our days in Nagrok life seemed to acquire a peculiar character of unreality, a sort of dream from which you could wake up at any moment but which held you none the less in the grip of the here and now—a here and now that was frightening and totally confusing. Even everyday smells and the colours of the landscape seemed to have changed a little, and once familiar sounds now had a strange ring to them. This can't be true, I thought. It will only last for a while, and then I will wake up and find John next to me and I will be back in our lovely home, the children will be playing in the garden and life will be once more uncomplicated and simple. Looking back forty-five years later I realise now that because our lives were in constant danger and our situation was likely to change suddenly, we lived intensely for every moment. And the moment was filled with fear.

After the unconditional surrender by the Dutch and before the Japanese Army could impose the new order and new rules, there was for a short time total confusion. The Dutch East Indies Army personnel had been confined to barracks and then locked up in prison camps. The civilian men who were still free, stayed home to protect their families. About four months later they too were rounded up and confined to special civilian prison camps.

In my case, we did not see a Japanese soldier until a couple of weeks after the fall of the government. I recall standing near our cottage and looking up towards the road where two army trucks loaded with Japanese soldiers were going by, their flag flying triumphantly. I froze. My hand went around my throat and I thought my heart would stop. Quickly regaining my composure, I gathered my children around me and, with Georgette and her baby, went inside and closed the doors. We debated what we should do and concluded that the only sensible thing was to lie low and be as inconspicuous as possible. The cottage was not visible from the road, being so far below and surrounded by dense foliage.

The news about the situation until then had been unreliable and controversial, as

immediately after the surrender all Dutch Radio broadcasts were banned. Proclamations and orders were broadcast in English, which the Dutch understood, but the rest of the news was in Japanese or Indonesian, neither of which were generally understood. Minsha possessed a big old radio and she kept us informed—until it became a crime to have one in the house. All radios were confiscated and there were severe penalties for possessing one. Some risked their lives by secretly listening in to sets they kept hidden and furtively conveying the news to their friends. Rumours, of course, were rife, and right from the beginning there were whispers about imminent secret landings by Allied troops intending to form a bridgehead from which to attack the Japanese and deliver us all. It was only wishful thinking and the unconscious desire to maintain morale—but the rumours continued right to the end of the three and a half year occupation.

We were afraid we might be discovered by the Japanese soldiers who roamed through the villages looking for food and women, and we were not optimistic about our chances if they stumbled upon our group of two European women and four children.

On one occasion we were almost discovered. One morning I heard voices calling out in Japanese and through the kitchen window saw two soldiers coming down the path from the main road. This is it, I thought, and cold sweat broke out on me. At the same time, however, I saw the slight figure of Atik coming out of his hut and blocking their path. He was gesticulating wildly; turning around, he pointed to our bungalow. The next moment the soldiers turned and made their way back to the road.

A moment later Atik stood in our doorway, slightly nervous but looking relieved as he explained that the Japanese had bought a chicken from a stall at the roadside (stolen, Atik assured me) and, wanting to clean it, they started down the path, intending to wash it in the water of the ricefields. Atik warned them that down there in the bungalow was a very sick person and he mentioned the plague. In an instant the soldiers were in retreat.

17

I often marvelled at Atik and Tjètjè's care for us. They hardly knew us, but they had placed us under their protection. I am sure that the small children and the fact that I was pregnant appealed to their paternal instincts: they were both dedicated husbands and fathers. We were helpless and utterly vulnerable, and their attitude towards us was impeccable. We could converse easily, as I spoke fluent Indonesian—communication that was invaluable.

Shortly after the episode with the Japanese soldiers and the chicken, Atik came to the cottage one day towards evening. He was greatly disturbed and explained to me that, due to the inadequacy of the native police force, bands of criminals were roaming the countryside. Amongst them, he said, were some crazed individuals who were *mata-gelap* (literally, *dark-eyed*) and who would try to destroy or maim or kill anything and anyone that stood in their way. He was very anxious to let me know that he and his brother would see that no harm would come to us. He then had to go back quickly to the families' huts to make sure that his younger brothers took charge of the women and children in his absence.

Just before dark the brothers installed themselves outside our bungalow in front of the two doors. It was a full moon that evening. Atik sat on a mat in front of the verandah door, a thin blanket around his shoulders and a long *klewang* (Indonesian sword) on his lap, while Tjètjè kept guard at the side door leading to the separate bathroom and kitchen. He also had a *klewang* at his side and they both assured me that the criminals would only get to us over their dead bodies.

The small oil lamp was on the floor near the mattresses. The children were asleep, thank God, and Georgette and I sat on cushions on the floor, listening for any suspicious noises close by outside. We could hear menacing screams in the distance and saw flames leaping up against the night sky. Revolver in hand, I sat contemplating what I had to do, if necessary. Shoot the intruders? I only knew that we must not fall alive into the hands of the madmen. I prayed and prayed and watched the sleeping children in the half-light.

After a long while—it seemed an eternity—we heard some shots, after which the screams appeared to diminish; gradually they died down. I went outside, still clasping the revolver, and talked to my two friends. They had just spoken to a messenger from a nearby village who told them that at a crucial moment the police had arrived and shot dead the ringleaders. He also said that the village, which lay between us and the marauding bands, was a 'good' village, the people incorruptible, so the criminals would be unable to recruit any weak elements there.

I was very moved by the brothers' loyalty.

They went to their homes, and I turned off the lamp, and sat in my chair on the verandah, moonlight streaming through the windows across the floor, reflecting on the way human beings are brought together in times of great danger and great need.

About six weeks after our arrival in Nagrok an incredible thing happened. It was early afternoon, and hot, and the children were having their afternoon nap. Georgette was hanging out the washing on the line strung between two trees and I sat on the edge of the mattress mending some clothes. Suddenly I heard the purring sound of a light motorbike on the road above. That was strange, as the only sound of motor traffic had been from the occasional truck loaded with Japanese soldiers. Next I heard footsteps coming down the path and, before I realised what was happening, a man in uniform stood in the open doorway. It was John, and for a moment I thought I was experiencing a vivid daydream brought on by my longing for him, but the next moment I was in his arms and he was real. The children woke up and we were sitting on the mattress, hugging each other and crying for joy. Georgette came in and joined in the unrestrained happiness of the moment. After some time John was able to tell us how he managed to make the journey. It was a miraculous story, an adventure which only someone as imaginative as John could have embarked upon.

Because the surrender by the Dutch East Indies government was unconditional, no further defensive fighting was possible and the troops had to lay down their arms and be taken into custody. The military garrison place of Tjimahi, near Bandung, was transformed into one great prison camp and it was there that John and his colleagues had ended up. He was in despair, as he did not know if the children and I had survived the traumatic transition to Japanese rule and he was frantic to find a means of contacting me. The driver of the car we had come in to Sukabumi duly returned and reported to his boss, who in turn contacted John, who then knew we had arrived safely at Hotel Salabintana. Feeling helpless and inactive in the prison camp, he began plotting how he could get out and find us.

He heard that the Japanese commander needed expert advice regarding the repair of a small strategic bridge which had previously been destroyed by the Dutch troops. He went to the office and offered to help, on condition that he would be able to leave the camp and investigate in person the extent of the damage. At first he was gruffly rebuffed, but it was decided on second thoughts to let him have a try.

Accompanied by a Japanese driver, John left the camp in a jeep. When he came to the bridge he pretended to investigate the damage and scribbled in his notebook. He bluffed his way through the next half hour, convinced the driver he had to ring some workshops for material (after all he was the expert and the poor driver spoke only broken English) and was able to give the man the slip. Using back alleys, he managed to reach the house of a friend of ours, where he found a young son home whom he persuaded to lend him his motorbike. Together they set off towards Sukabumi. However, there was a problem that seemed insurmountable. To leave the municipality of Bandung a pass had to be obtained, stamped by the Japanese authorities which allowed the bearer to proceed and granted access to the nominated destination. At a small office on the outskirts of Bandung soldiers with rifles at the ready stood guard on both sides of the road leading to Sukabumi.

John hopped off the motorbike and resolutely entered the wooden building which was packed with people wanting passes. The Japanese officer in charge was sitting behind a large desk, busily stamping the flimsy pieces of paper. John knew that how he acted in the next few moments was crucial. Feeling a rush of energy—he later wondered where the audacity came from—he brushed some people aside, and stood facing the Japanese officer who looked up, surprised, his stamping instrument held suspended in mid-air. Looking straight at the officer, John quickly demanded: 'Please, permission for six hours to go to Sukabumi and back.' He placed the piece of paper he had obtained to leave the prison camp that morning right in front of the officer, who brought the stamp down with a thud. Allowing the man no time to recover from this unexpected and authoritative behaviour, John quickly saluted and left the building. After showing his pass to the guards, he and his young friend set off on the bike for Sukabumi, about two hours away.

At Hotel Salabintana John was directed to our cottage in Nagrok. To ride so far on a motorbike in uniform—even though the signs of officer's rank had all been removed—without being apprehended was against all odds. His daring paid off and now he was with us, looking at us all with intensity, as if he wanted to print on his memory forever the way he saw us at that moment. We would not see each other again until Christmas 1945, more than three and a half years away, although we did not know that then of course. We spoke optimistically about the Allies certainly not letting us down and about it being only a question of time before we would be together once more.

John was obviously relieved that I was healthy, the traumatic experiences notwithstanding, and he lovingly stroked my belly and predicted an adventurous child. He gave me some money he had been able to

23

collect before he left the prison camp and then he hugged and kissed us all and disappeared as quietly as he had come. A moment later we heard the motorbike start up and we listened as the sound gradually disappeared into the distance. Atik and Tjètjè came down to share the excitement at my husband's sudden appearance—they thought him very brave. When he arrived back in the prison camp, they gave him a beating, but they were also relieved that he had returned to custody. The Japanese commander was most disappointed that the bridge appeared to be beyond repair, something that John knew would be the case even before he had seen it—he had no intention of playing into Japanese hands.

As my pregnancy advanced it sometimes became difficult for me to walk up the path to the road, especially if heavy rains had made it muddy and slippery. Minsha had a bungalow we could stay in and she urged me to leave our little house that had become quite dear to me and live on her premises.

My brother Bill and his family had left Hotel Salabintana by this time and they were living in the larger of Minsha's two bungalows. It seemed the best solution to live together as closely as possible during those uncertain times so we gratefully accepted Minsha's generous offer. Our new abode was certainly more convenient and comfortable than our simple cottage among the ricefields and Atik and Tjètjè who had been worried about my advanced condition, felt that I was safer in the hands of the very capable Minsha. We saw them every day, as they both worked in the big garden around Minsha's place. I still had a soft spot for the little white cottage and whenever it had not been raining for a few days I would go down and visit my beautiful friends who had stood by me during some very anxious weeks.

CHAPTER THREE

About four weeks after we moved in to Minsha's bungalow the order came that everyone had to be registered. We were required to go on a certain day to the local government office (in our case, the school for Indonesian children) to register our name, address, age, race and other statistical information. We were also required to state how much cash we had in our possession. The banks had been closed since the day of surrender. I cannot recall exactly how much money we were allowed to have, but it was certainly not much; from the Japanese point of view we European women would not need much cash, as we were destined to be rounded up with our children, and transported to civilian prison camps.

25

It was agreed that Minsha's aged mother and I would not attend the registration, as the very old, the very young and women in advanced pregnancy were allowed to stay home. The walk was quite long and strenuous, as the school was on the far side of a steep hill.

I rose before daybreak on that special morning in order to make everybody an early cup of coffee before they set off. Softly, so as not to wake up the children with whom I shared a bedroom, I went out and closed the door behind me. I had to walk across a concrete hallway towards the tiny kitchen outside, which was on a slightly lower level. It was still dark and a lamp lit the steps leading down. I still do not know what caused me to lose my balance as I put my foot on the first step—perhaps the light threw a tricky shadow. I tripped and, heavy and clumsy as I was by then, could not find a foothold. Down I went—first the few steps to the platform next to the kitchen and then, there being no railing to grab on to, down the twenty stone steps that led into the garden. Fully aware of what was happening, I saw myself as a very big bag of potatoes slowly tumbling down all those steps, at one stage upside down. I held my arms around my heavy stomach in a desperate attempt to shield the baby from injury. At last I landed in the garden with my head on the bottom step, the sharp stone edge of which had gashed my forehead between the eyes, causing it to bleed profusely. I immediately prodded to feel if the baby was still all right and was flooded with relief when I felt it kicking away merrily.

Georgette, in the other bedroom with her baby, was already up and changing the little girl when she heard me stumble and fall. She called out to ask if I was all right and was alarmed and terrified when my voice came from down in the garden. 'I am okay. Don't worry,' I said. Calling to the others she came rushing out, and they all stood at the top of the steps, looking down in horror at the still figure lying on the garden path. They rushed down to help me but I told them I wanted to lie very still for a moment and that I was completely unhurt. Slowly I got up after a time and was helped to the top of the steps.

I had been extremely lucky, with no damage to the baby, as far as we could determine, and no broken bones. My only injuries were the wound to my forehead, a badly cut knee and a stiff neck. I walked around with my head bowed for about a week—it was miraculous that I had not broken my neck. Although they did not betray their concern the others were worried that the fall may have affected the baby. Consequently when, some time later and more than a week before the due birthdate, I showed the first signs of labour, I was urged not to wait but to go immediately to the small missionary hospital I had booked into at

Sukabumi. My friend Apit, the taxi driver, was on hand to help. I had met him a few times as he was a friend of Atik and Tjètjè and did some odd jobs around the big house and the bungalows. His very important assets were an old battered taxi-cab and a small stone house not far from Nagrok on the way down to Sukabumi. Like his friends, he was very concerned about us women. I will never forget a day when we were having a cup of tea at his home. He wanted to tell us something and apparently was unsure how to go about it. He lifted his head to look at us and his eyes were misty as he said: 'When the day comes that the ladies will have to vacate their house and deliver all their money to the Japanese rulers, then they have to come to Apit's place and live here, and Apit and his family will occupy once more the old wooden hut behind this one and as long as there is corn and rice in his fields, so long there will be food for all of us.'

The Japanese had confiscated for military uses any cars they could lay their hands on, Minsha's included, but Apit kept his old taxi hidden behind some thick bushes and high trees. He had a tin of petrol in his shed and assured me he would use it to drive me down to the hospital when my time came. He also knew that he would lose his car when he brought it out of hiding. He was content as long as he could be of assistance in taking me down the steep road to Sukabumi.

It happened exactly as planned. The whole family and Atik and Tjètjè, the servants, and my other Indonesian friends, all stood in the front garden waving goodbye while the old car, creaking a bit in protest, started on the road down. Apit was grinning with satisfaction that we were moving and I leaned back and held on to the seat and to my little suitcase.

Halfway down we stopped, where as agreed, a horse and cart was waiting at the side of the road. I was transferred to the cart and, at a signal from the driver, the horse set off willingly on the last few kilometres down the path to the town. Apit turned back with his car, trying not to be too conspicuous, but the ruling masters saw him and took away his precious possession.

At the missionary hospital I was taken to a bed in a room with two other women, one of whom had already given birth. As it turned out, the labour pains had been a false alarm. I stayed in the hospital, however, as it was a safe place to be.

A week later the labour started again, this time in earnest, and four hours later my healthy baby girl was born. Amid the strains of a war song from Japanese soldiers marching by in the street below, the doctor—a gentle, motherly woman—held up my child for me to see and said: 'What a lovely baby, she has dimples in her cheeks.' So many feelings rushed through me: joy at having this child

29

after all we had gone through together, sorrow at not being able to share this moment with John. And where was he? Was he alive? How long would it be before we would be reunited? But the overriding feeling was of gratitude and the ever-new experience of wonder, when with the soft bundle in my arms I breathed in the lovely smell of a newborn baby.

I called her Nelleke. This was the name written on a piece of paper that had been smuggled out of John's prison camp and that reached me a few weeks after his visit. It was his nickname for me—he must have sensed that our fourth child was going to be a girl. I had been able to keep in touch with my family

in Nagrok, as Minsha was allowed to keep her phone for the benefit of her First Aid post. Now I rang and told them the happy news. As it was advisable for Europeans not to show their faces unnecessarily in the streets—the atmosphere was threatening and frightening— we decided that they would remain on the mountain rather than risk coming down to visit me.

The mission doctor was a most generous woman and I was allowed to pay no more than a token amount of money. Thirty-five years later I met her again when I traced her whereabouts to a retirement village in Holland. We spent a moving time together, reminiscing about a very eventful past.

When it was time for me to leave the hospital my sister-in-law came down from Nagrok in a horse and cart to get me. When the long, slow journey back up the mountain was almost over, a little group of people came out to greet us at the side of the road. Atik, Tjètjè and Apit and several more Indonesian friends were all there, and of course many children. With flowers and paper streamers they had decorated a cane chair and lashed it to two long bamboo poles. I sat down in it and four men lifted the poles on to their shoulders and in triumph carried me the last couple of kilometres to the big house, surrounded by singing, dancing children, their families, my sister-in-law and well-wishing strangers.

31

I was blinded by tears, and hid my face against Nelleke's soft downy head. In the driveway to the house my children, my brother and his children, Georgette and her baby, Minsha and many more were assembled to give me an unforgettable 'welcome'. This was a royal homecoming I could never have imagined.

After four weeks I had to return to Sukabumi for a check-up. Nelleke had her 10 o'clock feed before I set off, and I was sure I would be back four hours later to feed her again. It was beautiful weather, there was a cool mountain breeze, and I knew I could make the journey on foot if I was unable to hail a *doccar* (horse and cart). As it turned out there were no carts to be had, so I was rather tired and dusty when I arrived at the hospital.

The friendly doctor gave me a drink and something to eat—and also a clean bill of health. At a shop I bought some baby powder and a bag of sweet biscuits for the children, but I noticed the town was subdued and uneasy. The presence of so many Japanese soldiers in the streets and the absence of the usual crowds made me uncomfortable, so I was glad to get out of the town and on the road home to Nagrok. I looked around the market place on the edge of the town in vain for a *doccar* to take me up the mountain. I started walking, but hoped that sooner or later I would come across a vacant cart.

It was past midday and the heat was scorching. The ricefields stretched out on both sides of the road, the heat haze obscuring the horizon. Now and then I stopped for a while in the shade of a tree. The birds were silent, having all retreated into the cool foliage. I exchanged friendly greetings with the few Indonesian men and women I encountered along the road, but I had to refuse the smiling offers of a cold drink and a chair to rest in awhile. I knew that I had to be back in Nagrok in time for Nelleke's next feed. No *doccar* came in sight and I realised that I had to go all the way on foot.

My breasts were practically bursting with milk, and I did not know if I could keep up the pace on the gradually steepening road, when I had a strange experience. It was the first of several I encountered over the years at times when the going was really tough and there was no obvious solution. Suddenly I felt I was being supported; the weight of my body pressing down on my weary feet was relieved to a large degree and the going became effortless. I felt I had been hooked up to a source of energy which infused me with new strength, a kind of reserve tank that had been there all the time. And the tank was limitless. It was an exhilarating feeling, and by the time I reached Nagrok and walked up the driveway, I felt at peace and grateful to have been granted the experience.

When Nelleke was forty days old, I gave a big *selamatan* (feast) for the Indonesian children in the neighbourhood and their parents. Atik had told me about the legend concerning the village of Nagrok in which mention was made of the birth of a white child who would take all bad luck away and make it into a prosperous place. So he thought it desirable that a Muslim priest be invited who would intone the appropriate prayers to ask for a happy and long life for Nelleke and the much-needed prosperity for the village.

They all tried to assemble in the loungeroom of our bungalow, but of course there was a spillover on to the cement deck and into the garden. Everyone sat on the floor, the little ones in front; I sat on a chair, with Nelleke on my lap, where they could all see her while the priest spoke the sacred words. A pair of swallows came flying in, dipped down over the congregation, and flew out again. It was explained to me that this was an auspicious sign, and that it rarely happened. When it was time at the end for the distribution of the festive meal, everyone filed out, each reverently holding the delicacies, neatly packaged in folded banana leaves.

About a week later Georgette and I decided to pursue a risky plan. I so much wanted to try to get a glimpse of John and to show him our little Nelleke that I was prepared to make the train trip from Sukabumi to Bandung and from there get to the big military prison camp in Tjimahi. Georgette, whose husband was interned with John, also wanted to come with her baby and we both knew the risks we were taking. The trains ran irregularly and we could not foresee what difficulties lay ahead of us.

We departed very early one morning. The train carriage was packed and we were conspicuous because few European women were around. Minsha had given us an address of a friend in Bandung where, if necessary, we could stay the night. After arriving at Bandung station, however, we were lucky to get seats on a little old bus which took us, together with some other passengers, to Tjimahi.

A few years before, John and I had lived at Tjimahi when it was an army garrison, so I knew my way around the barracks. They were all converted now into large compounds surrounded by wire fences strengthened by barbed wire. We could see prisoners walking around or sitting in groups. Keeping an eye on the Japanese guards who were stationed at intervals along the perimeter, we very carefully inched closer to the fence at a point where some bushes would hide us.

A couple of prisoners had discovered us and came ambling towards the fence, pretending they wanted to smoke a cigarette in the shade. We held up our babies and when they were within earshot, we mentioned our husbands' names and the battalion they were connected

35

with. One shook his head sadly and told us that very early that morning trainloads of prisoners, including that battalion, had departed for Jakarta, from where they would be transported to Singapore. It was very hard to accept that we had missed our men by only a few hours, and we realised that our trains probably passed each other on the way.

By the time we arrived at Minsha's friend's house in Bandung it was getting dark, so we were very grateful to have a place where we could lie down and have a meal. We were both exhausted, physically and emotionally. We reached Sukabumi the next afternoon. On our way up the mountain, a wild thunderstorm broke and the rain lashed the brave little horse and soaked us as we huddled in the cart with our babies behind flimsy oilskin covers. When the road became too steep for the horse to pull us any further, we had to alight but fortunately the tropical storm had just finished—as suddenly as it had started. Brilliant sunshine warmed and dried us and sparkled in the thousands of raindrops hanging from the leaves and glittering in the grass. Steam rose from the road and the sight of all that luxurious growth after so heavy a downpour gladdened my heart.

It happened a few times that Japanese soldiers came up the mountain. They generally drove jeeps, and when we heard a vehicle stop and loud voices and heavy footsteps approach the house, we immediately gathered our children around us like a first line of defence. We had experienced how the sight of children softened the hearts of these soldiers—they often knelt down beside the children, offered them sweets (if they had them) and stroked their heads. Discipline in the Japanese army was harsh. 'Fraternising' was forbidden and if a soldier tried to molest a woman he could be shot on the spot. These rules came into effect after the first few unsettled months, during which many atrocities and rapes were committed by the stormtroops.

In the beginning we were terrified when we heard a car or a jeep coming up the driveway and coming to a stop with a loud squeal of the brakes. But when we realised that providing some food and drink was all that was expected of us, it was no longer such a nightmare. Sometimes a soldier wanted to have a wash; he would take all his clothes off, ask for a towel and disappear into the bathroom.

At these times we women found strength in numbers and we always stayed close together, occasions when my brother and Minsha's husband were hiding in a cupboard or under the bed. It happened time and time again that a few of the soldiers would show us photos of their wives and children that they kept in their wallets. In broken English and sometimes with gestures they would tell us they had not seen them for months or more often years. They often sat down on the floor with our children and just looked at them.

The civilian men were gradually rounded up and taken to special prison camps. It was hard to say goodbye to my brother Bill, although we all wanted to keep up a brave front. It was good that we did not know then that more than three years would pass before we would meet again.

CHAPTER FOUR

After the civilian men had been taken away to the prison camps, mostly on Java, the European women and children began being herded together and camps were prepared for them in most major cities. Our little group was destined for Bandung, the second largest city in West Java after Jakarta. Several residential blocks in an outlying suburb of the city had been set aside for women and children from as far away as Sukabumi.

Nelleke was about four or five months old when we left Sukabumi for the Kareës prison camp in Bandung—the time was October or November 1942. I remember clearly how uncertain and unprotected we felt after the men left. We knew that our time of relative freedom would soon be replaced by total confinement. Our Indonesian friends were full

of compassion and I remember Atik trying to keep up with the slow moving bus which departed from Minsha's driveway. He had tears in his eyes and wanted to say something but was unable. He held on to my hand through the window as long as his swift-running feet would let him. Minsha and her children and the old grandmother stood huddled together, shocked and tearful at our departure. They were still free, being German, but Minsha's Dutch husband had already been imprisoned and they were fearful and uncertain about the future. Eventually, after the war, they were reunited and spent the rest of their lives in Holland.

My sister-in-law and her children and Georgette and her baby were also on the bus, which was a great comfort, and I had also met some of the other passengers before. As we drove down the mountain in the old creaking bus, we picked up more people destined for Sukabumi, from where we would be transported by train to Bandung.

The terminal at Sukabumi was the former primary school for Dutch-speaking children, which was now closed as European education was no longer allowed. For the one night we stayed there we were allocated a small space in one of the classrooms where we slept on mats on the floor. It was most uncomfortable and I remember being very worried about Nelleke, who had a high fever as a result of an infected smallpox inoculation. She cried a lot and the other children felt threatened by the uncertainty, so we all huddled together for comfort.

The next morning we were taken in buses to trains waiting at the railway station. We formed quite a crowd, more and more people having arrived at the school from different plantations around Sukabumi. There were also several elderly civilian gentlemen, most of them retired, who had been allowed to stay with their wives. However, after living in the women's prison camp for some time (it was about a year, I think) they were taken away to join the younger men in the male civilian camps.

When we arrived at Kareës prison camp, it appeared that many people had already been allocated houses. To my delight there were tree-lined streets in this part of Bandung and most of the houses looked friendly and some had attractive gardens. As might be imagined, not much of these gardens remained after a while, and the grass nature-strips were trampled bare by the hundreds upon hundreds of people herded there. The hundreds later swelled to thousands.

I was taken with the four children to a house of average size, where I was allocated a rather large room. Installing myself on the few mattresses provided, I tried to make Nelleke comfortable and feed her (fortunately her high temperature had subsided by this time). I kept Peter on the mattress with me—he was twenty months old—and he quickly fell asleep. My older ones—Johnny, almost five, and Manya, three and a half, were much too excited by this adventure to stay with me. They slipped out of the room to explore the little backyard and then went to the front and sat on the low stone wall to watch the passers-by. I had given them strict orders not to walk on to the street and every now and then I went outside and checked up on them. They were overwhelmed by all the people crowding the streets and yards.

The number of children was astonishing—certainly a sight to get used to. For my children this was a mixed blessing. On the one hand they were delighted to have so many playmates. There was never a dull moment for them and they all shared happily the few toys that we had been able to include in our luggage. On the other hand, as is inevitable in any crowd, there were a few very aggressive children who sought to lord it over the younger ones, damage their precious toys and even beat them up.

My sister-in-law, Karsia, and her children were assigned to a much larger building than mine, not far from where Georgette and her baby shared a room with a friend from Nagrok and her two children. The area of the camp was not large, and they were only a short walk away from my place.

The camp was ruled by an office of Japanese administrators, where Indonesians filled the clerical positions. Then followed the Dutch 'camp-leader', a very capable young woman who was responsible for the whole community, a daunting task, in view of the unsolvable problems that often presented themselves. She had an admirable flair for acting as go-between in tricky situations that developed in the camp; she was also fearless, and the Japanese had a deep respect for courage.

I was the 'house-leader' of our place where twenty people resided (with only one bathroom and one toilet and severe water restrictions). Between the levels of camp-leader and house-leader was the 'street-leader', who had the often thankless task of keeping the peace in the street and was responsible for any breach of rules. It was an enormous organisation to run smoothly on all the aspects of health, the problems of overcrowding and physical and mental distress concerning about 10,000 displaced people. We women did not have much direct contact with the Japanese, as the Dutch camp-leader and the several street-leaders acted as the intermediaries. But sometimes a Japanese official or a soldier walked through the camp on a special investigation or to follow up a community complaint.

Often it was difficult to judge how to react to the Japanese. Most often, when they encountered courage they showed their appreciation, but sometimes they reacted angrily, with disastrous consequences for the victim. I was once in a situation in which I threw caution to the wind and let my indignation overrule my normal sense of restraint. One day into 'our' garden came a Japanese in uniform; he was responding to a complaint made on behalf of our house. Just what this complaint was I can no longer recall. I do know, however, that trying to get some essential service repaired had been very annoying and long drawn out; perhaps it entailed the water pipes or some such inconvenience. Whatever it was, the Japanese man at last had come to investigate. As house-leader I felt responsible for the welfare of my group and, forgetting to bow for him, I immediately started to tackle him about the long neglect of the office in attending to the problem. I cannot remember what language I spoke to him, but he became very flustered and mumbled something in broken English. When I stopped my tirade (I realised that I had let myself get carried away into a dangerous situation), he saluted, bowed and marched out of the garden. Shortly afterwards a few Indonesian workers came to repair the faulty system.

Food distribution was a gigantic

organisation. There were a few large communal kitchens where the women had to take turns helping to cut up vegetables or assisting with the cleaning and cooking. There was a skeleton staff of permanent workers who chopped the wood for the big ovens, lit the fires and kept them going, stirred the big pots and ladled out the soup and rice at mealtimes. These were generally women who had no young children; the mothers of small children worked to a roster. Looking back on that period I marvel at the efficiency and hard work involved in organising that huge community under such difficult and fearsome circumstances.

The Japanese leaders were content to leave the actual running of the camp to the Dutch organisers but were always ready to pounce whenever there was a breach of their rules. We had to be counted twice every day, morning and evening. If there was one person short, the authorities would not let up until she had been accounted for. Trying to escape met with dire punishment.

The fences around the camp were made of tightly woven bamboo; they were very high and topped by barbed wire. At regular intervals in watchtowers were Indonesian guards armed with rifles and tommy-guns. At night powerful lights shone on the perimeter. It was amazing that occasionally some hastily scribbled items of news from outside reached us. These were

45

obtained by daring women in the camp, generally those without children, who ran great risks by doing so. Sometimes they received the news orally by walking close to the fence where a friend or paid messenger on the other side mumbled a few words. The scraps of paper were smuggled in when the big gates opened to let in the food trucks and were destroyed immediately they were received.

The news that eventually reached the inmates of the camp became distorted, assuming an optimistic turn. So strong was the belief that the war would soon be over that every bit of news was seen as a step further towards liberation. The belief that things were very bad then but it wouldn't be long before life was back to normal turned out to be a life-saver for many. Eternal optimism in times of deepest depression was something I saw everywhere around me. When I look back on it, I realise what a hopeful sign it is that man— that woman—has the adaptability to be resilient in the face of disaster.

One great consolation was that we were all suffering the same fate and so could easily relate to each other's woes and miseries and seek solace in each other's understanding. And we realised that this suffering was common to those outside as well as inside the camp. People were still arriving from outlying districts and from them we heard about circumstances in other camps and about the uncomfortable situation of the Eurasian people who had been allowed to stay outside. Often their lives were precarious, their 'freedom' curtailed by anxiety—especially among women who lived on their own—as robbery and house-breaking were rife. Several women of mixed Dutch and Indonesian descent or of Dutch-Chinese origin managed to get into our camp under the pretext of being related to prisoners.

Friendships were readily formed and help from other members of the household or from neighbours was crucial in times of sickness or grief, especially when it concerned the children. I would never have thought it possible that there could be laughter in a prison camp, but laugh we did, many a time at silly situations or the latest joke, or sometimes we would suddenly see the humour in a grim happening. It was a theatre of tragi-comedy and it was larger than life.

The instinct for survival in the face of increasing threats of starvation, intolerable overcrowding and ultimate annihilation brought certain character traits in people to the fore. It seemed that people who were selfish and showed disregard for the welfare of others became more greedy, while their sisters-in-prison who were willing to share and show consideration for others became even more so. The threat to our survival highlighted our personalities.

Some hidden talents were discovered too by the sheer necessity of improving the quality of our lives. Although obtaining sufficient food was of the greatest importance, I think that many of us felt that we could not live by bread alone. Especially for the children it was important that some of the niceties of life be preserved. There were no shops in the camp where we could buy any toys to celebrate birthdays, but it was inspiring and impressive to see mothers fashion some lovely things from rags, pieces of wood or small tins that we found under the houses—the leftovers of the people who had once lived normal lives here. Women who considered they had no artistic ability surprised themselves by creating some original and beautiful pieces. The discovery of this potential was exciting and often seemed to help us cope better with the worsening conditions.

At the very beginning it was still possible to obtain some items from outside the camp. Visitors were occasionally allowed in and a distant relative of mine brought me some thin coloured cardboard and a few tubes of water paint and brushes. At my request, and shortly before these visits were forbidden, she brought me a small wooden truck, simply fashioned and bought at the local market. I hid it so that Johnny, whose birthday it was for, could not discover it and I worked on it whenever the children were playing outside or were asleep. I made it into a Red Cross truck: one woman had given me an old piece of white sheeting and with great patience I sewed tiny little bags and filled them up with sand, little pebbles, grass seeds and anything I could find that seemed interesting. I painted red crosses on them and on the truck, and tiny red crosses on the veils of the nursing sisters and on the driver and his mate, which I had made from cottonwool, sticks and sheeting. When it was finished, the night before his birthday, I was very pleased with it and felt there could not be a better Red Cross truck in all the world. The next morning, after we had sung the birthday song, the truck was unveiled amid great exclamations of wonder and excitement.

After breakfast the three older children went to play while I tidied the room and fed Nelleke. After some time I heard a muffled cry, and Johnny stood in the room, the dismantled and partly broken truck in his hands. Manya and Peter and some of their friends crowded around him. A big bully in the street had grabbed the truck and used it as a football. It took me a long time to console him—after all, he was only five.

CHAPTER FIVE

The coloured cardboard, paint and brushes my relative had brought me gave me great pleasure. I had always loved drawing and painting, and now I decided to try to turn that ability into a source of income, however modest. The money would enable me to buy a few little extras for the children. Every now and then special food arrived at the camp—bananas, cookies and lollies, for instance, which were distributed to each street for sale. They were cheap, I remember, but if you did not have the cash you missed out. Some women who managed to bring money with them into the camp were always able to buy these items which brought some colour and extra flavour to our monotonous, drab menus.

I decided to make calendars. On to the coloured cardboard I pasted a picture I painted, and underneath the picture the tiny calendar I had painstakingly made, month by month; it was sewn together with cotton thread. The finished product was rather attractive and I sold a good many (of course I could charge only very little) and with the money bought the greatly desired sweet luxuries. The sale of these delicacies was stopped after about six months. Coincidentally at this time I sold my last calendar—having used up my supply of paper and paint.

The calendar making had been done mostly at night. The days were taken up by looking after the children, washing clothes, tidying up and doing my share of community work which did not amount to much when Nelleke was still a baby. But the trouble was that we were not allowed to have the lights on at night after a certain rather early hour. So I saw to it that the curtains were hermetically drawn and, shading my little reading lamp with a book, I worked on my project often until late at night.

On one of these evenings, with the children as usual fast asleep, it was absolutely quiet and I busied myself preparing the paints. A woman had ordered two calendars and she wanted specific paintings on each of them. One had to depict her elderly mother who was fond of playing the accordion for her two grandchildren, and the other was intended for her sister-in-law who had been a gourmet cook. This was a daunting assignment as I generally painted old-fashioned girls in frilly finery, sometimes with handsome suitors. But the prospect of more cash coming in encouraged me. I had the pencil poised above the paper and remember glancing at the little clock on my desk. And then . . . nothing!

What happened in the next few hours I have no idea. When I awoke with a start I thought I must have fallen asleep, as I had been tired. Looking at the clock I realised that three hours had elapsed. Then I saw two pictures in front of me on the table—two exquisite little pictures. One was of a grandmother sitting on a log in a forest playing her accordion, while sitting on the ground, looking up at her were a boy and girl. The other showed an elegant lady in the kitchen, with a recipe book in hand, stirring a pot on the stove. Both were of the most beautiful pastel shades and finished in the finest detail. It was the work of a professional artist, which I was not, although it was impossible that anyone else could have done the work. I was in awe of the paintings in front of me and totally puzzled by them.

The next day I took the calendars to the lady who had ordered them. She was delighted. I regretted having to leave them with her as I would have loved to keep them as proof that miracles still happen. It made my world sparkle for days.

On another evening, a couple of months after we had arrived in the camp, I was reading the children a story before they went to sleep, when I heard a soft knocking on the door. I stopped in mid-sentence and listened intently. The knocking was repeated, this time a bit louder. I told the children to lie quietly and not to say a word while I tiptoed to the door. Frightening thoughts went through my head as we all had heard about unexpected night visits by the *kempetai* (secret police) who took away for questioning people who often never returned.

Holding the doorknob and keeping my voice steady, I asked: Who is there? 'This is Tjètjè, Nonja,' came the whispered reply. I could not believe my ears and quickly opened the door. There in the dark stood our good friend from Nagrok, his eyes riveted on my face. He carried a little suitcase. 'Tjètjè,' I said almost sobbing with relief and emotion as I pulled him swiftly inside and drew the curtains.

'Tjètjè, how did you get here, how did you know where I was?' I asked him, holding his hands in mine and searching his face which was lit up by a wide grin. He said, 'I wanted to see if you and the children were all right and I wanted to bring this suitcase which you left behind.' The little battered suitcase contained some clothes which I had had to leave behind in Minsha's bungalow when I left for the camp. It had worried Tjètjè ever since because he was convinced that the children and I would need the extra clothes. He obtained the address of the camp from Minsha and found it after quite a bit of searching. At a place where a tree grew near the fence and relying on the cover of the darkness, he climbed over the barbed wire. Craftily he hid himself behind bushes and crept down little back-streets until he found where I was.

He re-enacted the whole drama for us, much to our delight. He had always been the showman in the village and now our room was his stage. He had to keep his voice down, however, and there was much suppressed laughter. The children crowded around him and he stroked their heads and looked at each in turn. He took a bag of sweets from his pocket, placed it on the table and, looking up at me, said, 'I have to go now.' We held hands—I did not want to let him go—and then he disappeared into the night as quietly and mysteriously as he had arrived.

I was very moved by his courage and friendship and I still could not believe how he had located me. Perhaps the story of how he scaled the fence was just a cover-up and he had gained entry with the help of some sympathetic Indonesian guard at the gate. It was a great mystery. When at last, thirty years later, I returned to Indonesia to trace my good friends, I located Tjètjè's home and his family but Tjètjè had died the week before. But that is another story.

The dismal conditions in the camp, the overcrowding, the hunger and the fear took their toll of women who did not have the temperament to cope with the problems. They simply could not face the seemingly unending succession of drab, hungry days which they felt sure would end in their annihilation. This attitude showed in their complete lack of interest in what was happening in the camp. They became totally apathetic, letting their children, if they had any, collect the plates of food at mealtimes; and they lay listlessly on their mattresses while the children ate as best as they could on the floor or on the stone steps outside. Their friends tried to help the women by giving them courage, but it was often a thankless task, moreover, most mothers had their own hands full trying to cope with their own children and their own problems.

The crucial difference seemed to be what you believed in. Did the future hold no hope at all or was there some light, however dim, at the end of the long dark tunnel? I fiercely believed that one day we would be free, that the gates would open and we would all walk out. I was also convinced that the day would come upon us unexpectedly—as suddenly as the First World War had finished. Every time after Christmas had come and gone I was convinced that by Easter we would be free. When that proved wrong, I fixed my hopes on the next Christmas. Never once did I doubt that the bells of freedom would ring out for us, sooner or later.

I had a few arguments about this with a good friend of mine. She was an intellectual, sound-thinking woman who scoffed at my eternal optimism, as she called it. She was involved in the very risky business of obtaining news from outside and told me that, according to her information, there was not the slightest chance of the Allied forces coming to our help; the Allies were not faring at all well, she said, either in Europe or in the Pacific, and we would be left to rot, unimportant—there was no way out for us. She reproached me for deceiving myself with false optimism, and she could not understand my hopes. 'What future?' she would say. 'It would be much better if you could look reality in the eyes and accept the inevitable. And take that smile off your face.'

Maybe I was too naive to understand the workings of world politics or to accept that we were not important on the international stage—and I was blissfully ignorant of the possibility of a long-lasting dark night bearing down on us. When at last, on 15 August 1945, the Japanese surrendered and we were freed—indeed, unexpectedly—I was in a camp near Jakarta. There, a few weeks later, I met up with my friend, who was only a shell of her former self. She had given up long ago and she could barely accept a world she now faced with bitter suspicion. 'You were right and I was wrong,' she said. 'You were always able to laugh and believe the impossible. I thought I knew it all, but I left no room for even a grain of optimism. You look like you could tackle anything, but I feel empty and old.'

It was not that I had been ignorant of all the dangers and possible disasters that surrounded us, but I knew I had a choice about how I was going to react to them. I believed that by being positive and acting with hope I would gradually be led into ways which would turn out to be beneficial. I did not wrack my brains trying to understand my convictions—I just accepted that there was a guidance and surrendered totally to it.

This is why I was able to fall asleep at night as soon as I put my head on the pillow; I never lay awake plagued by thoughts of hopelessness and despair. And I needed any hour, any half hour of sleep that I could snatch, in between the children's bouts of coughing or tending them during illness, to survive. I too sometimes suffered from illness, but I was always able to carry on, no doubt because I could not bear to contemplate being too ill to mind the children.

Illness, or an attack of lice, or a punitive measure which made us all suffer, was sometimes very hard to bear. To remind myself of the conduct necessary to help me survive, I had written with chalk on the back of the wardrobe cum room divider: 'Mother, more patience, more gentleness, more love.'

I remember looking at these words over and over again on one occasion when I was very ill and confined to my mattress. I was in excruciating pain with an infected toe. A macabre blue line was creeping slowly towards my groin. Fortunately just then a friend was able to get hold of some Rivanol for me, a potent medication. After applying to the toe some rags saturated in the green liquid, the spreading infection was arrested, the pain became bearable, and after a few hours I was able to hobble around.

That was Christmas Day 1943. I was low in spirit that day, realising that yet another Christmas had arrived and we were still imprisoned, when something unexpectedly beautiful happened. The children had been playing in the yard, with the exception of Nelleke who was lying beside me having her afternoon nap. Manya came into the room and came straight to me. She bent over, kissed me on the cheek, on the tip of my nose, on my forehead, then looked deeply into my eyes and said 'Hullo'. Then off she went again to play. For that moment her eyes, big and dark like my husband's, had taken on John's expression, and she had kissed me in the special manner he used to say goodnight to me, a little ritual she had no knowledge of.

It was not the first time she had shown a strong psychic sense, unwittingly forming a bridge between John and me. The night before John had arrived in Nagrok on the motorbike, she sat up from her sleep and said clearly, 'Mummy, Daddy has been here and he said he will be coming soon,' and promptly fell asleep again. Her remarkable gesture on that Christmas Day very much helped me to carry on with new strength.

Strength was in great need as conditions in the camp deteriorated rapidly as more people came in and the houses became filled to capacity. One helpful factor in our predicament was the tropical climate. The overcrowding caused women and children to sleep out on verandahs and terraces. Although the nights in Bandung were sometimes chilly (there were no covers or extra clothing available), the days were mostly clear and warm and the bright sunshine cheered us up. It also supplied us with vitamin D and at any available opportunity I used to stretch out on the ground in the sun. I craved that warmth and I became incredibly brown, but I took care to cover my eyes with leaves. Unlike me, the children spent practically the whole day outside. Although they too were pitifully thin, they seemed to adapt surprisingly well to their fear-filled surroundings.

Being one of a team of four (Nelleke had grown up quickly and wanted to take part in their games) was a great advantage for the children. Whenever they were sick—and generally what one had they all got—they had each other to talk to, quarrel with or play games with. Their imagination was boundless, their energy surprising, but when a severe illness drained the precious strength from their emaciated bodies, they would lie listless and exhausted. My heart would beat anxiously as I watched them, trying not to contemplate the unthinkable. But time after time they rallied. So many other children around us died and

59

there was so much heartbreak.

During the first year the food situation was not too bad. The meals were small, simple and basic but hunger set in when the quantities began to shrink and the food became less nourishing.

I had tried to feed Nelleke with my own milk for as long as possible, but soon I had to give her a supplement. She did not seem to be able to digest properly the baby food provided by the communal kitchen—it was a semolina type of porridge—but from nine months she had to rely solely on that and an occasional banana. It was then the trouble started with vomiting and diarrhoea. At night I had to walk her around the room, crooning soothing words, so she would not wake up the others, until at last, totally exhausted, she would fall asleep. By her second birthday she was tolerating the food a little better.

She was very thin and not strong physically—she had not really had much chance of being strong from the beginning—but she was a little fighter. The energy of the life force seemed to have concentrated in her mental abilities. She was extraordinarily bright, could recite poems and sing songs when she was eighteen months and could also count, parrotwise, from one to twenty. Sitting on a cushion, thin and erect, with those big dark eyes in the heart-shaped face, she would repeat songs and sentences with the ease of a six-year-old. People came to watch in disbelief.

Johnny, the eldest, was tall for his age, and being naturally of slim build, was extremely thin. Manya did not become lean so soon, but with starvation becoming more common, her body also became emaciated. Only Peter seemed to withstand the onslaught on his health. He was sturdily built, and the teenage girls in the camp often pinched his muscular thighs and calves, as he looked so cuddly. He must have been about three when he fiercely bit on the bottom a much bigger boy who was attacking Johnny. Howling, the fellow let go of Johnny whereupon Peter, as fast as his little sturdy legs would carry him, set off with Johnny towards 'home'. I had arrived on the scene just in time to see the drama and sent the big boy packing with a few stern words.

Peter was only a shadow of his former strong self by the time the war ended. There was still a long way to go and many more agonies in store before then.

CHAPTER SIX

At the beginning of our time in Kareës prison camp, when the visitors were occasionally allowed in, some kind people brought us equipment they thought might be of use— items of furniture, for example. In this way I obtained Nelleke's little cot, a reading lamp, some chairs and a small desk. In a heap of goods I found an old typewriter and at my request a woman brought me a book about Dutch shorthand. Whenever I had a chance during the day I taught myself typing and at night I studied shorthand until I had mastered it. Later, after the war, I went to night classes in Holland and did exams in both subjects. When I held the certificates in my hand, I thought back to the turbulent times when I began my studies.

I also tried to improve my English, which I had studied for five years—it was a compulsory high school subject at schools in Holland and Dutch schools in Indonesia—and a dear English lady, the mother-in-law of one of my friends, gave me some lessons in exchange for one of my calendars. The effort of staying alive, tending the children and all the mundane tasks made me long to exercise my mind as much as possible.

To discipline myself and to make the most of the limited precious time I could use for my own purposes, I made a habit of allocating a certain time for each subject I intended to study. It may have been no longer than ten minutes at a time on occasions, but regularly, daily if possible. Each moment snatched from the household tasks brought elation, a feeling of triumph over restricting circumstances which would otherwise have prevented me

giving my spirit free reign.

I had brought a few children's books with me into the camp and we all exchanged whatever children's reading material we had. Before the children fell asleep at night I read them something or made up fairy stories in which they each had a role. In this way they could forget the rumblings of their hungry tummies and drift off into a fantasy world.

A certain degree of discipline was needed in this unnatural lifestyle. Normally not a very organised person, I saw to it that during mealtimes we sat together around the table and after a moment of silence we would eat the meagre helping of rice and watery vegetables that had been dished up in the communal kitchen. I had one white tablecloth, almost threadbare, which, together with an empty condensed milk tin containing some greenery or an occasional flower, gave us the feeling that civilised living was still possible.

As in ordinary life, friendships brought happiness and stimulation. Mart, who became my best friend, was introduced to me by a mutual acquaintance and from the first moment we met we felt an immediate rapport. We were the same height and of similar build and, although we could not see it ourselves, apparently we looked alike—so much so that people thought we were twins.

Mart had one child, a daughter of Peter's age, and towards evening after the last meal of the day, which was generally a repeat of 'lunch'—only less of it—she would come to my room while the children had one last game before bedtime. We talked and talked, told each other about our lives before Kareës, our husbands, the places we had lived. It was as if two best friends were at last reunited after a long separation. It is rare to find another being so compatible and rarer still to encounter this friend under such circumstances. Mart had a room in a house just around the corner from ours, and we often visited each other to talk and philosophise; in doing so we lightened each other's load.

We realised that in a way we were lucky our children were still small, especially in the case of boys. The Japanese office had quite a problem on its hands with boys in their mid-teens who entered the camp at the beginning with their mothers. They were rather assertive and the commander, fearing trouble, arranged for them to be sent elsewhere. These sixteen and seventeen year old young men apparently felt out of place in a camp crowded with women and small children. The Japanese also felt there would be complications from the sexual exploits of adventurous boys and lonely women. They saw the boys' removal as the only practical solution. They were sent away at a gradually younger age until by the end of 1943 ten-year-old boys were leaving their anguished mothers behind. What was going to happen to them? What sinister plan did the Japanese have in store for them?

The first time I heard about this practice was when a distraught mother came to my room and begged me to make a portrait of her young son who had to leave the camp in two days. From the beginning of Japanese rule it was decreed that no cameras were allowed; they were all confiscated, along with any radios. The mother had heard that I had drawn a few portraits for friends and of course I was happy to oblige her request. Several other boys found their way to my room, where they sat solemn-faced while I tried to sketch them as a consolation for their poor mothers. Most of the boys, however, seemed to look upon their move as a great adventure and as they climbed into the waiting trucks with their small bundles of belongings strapped to their backs, they even joked with each other—after all most of them were friends. And because they were so young, the Japanese guards did not treat them roughly but gave them a helping hand. There was no explanation given about what was going to happen to them. Understandably their mothers feared the worst. When the war was over, it turned out that the boys had been taken to civilian men's camps, where many of them had been reunited with fathers or older brothers. It would have given the mothers a certain peace of mind had they known this, but the absence of reliable information and the constant threat of harsh punishment for disobedience or disrespect produced unquestioning submission.

Rumours—always the rumours—had it that the men's camps were on Java and that none of the men had been taken overseas to Singapore or to Japan as we had also heard. Although evidence pointed to the fact that indeed great contingents of Dutch military had been shipped away from Indonesia, most women stubbornly believed that they were held in camps not far away from ours and that when the war came to an end, the gates would open and lo and behold, our loved ones would storm in to rescue us.

In my case (and many women had the same idea) I carefully kept aside a dress I had found abandoned in a wardrobe when we entered the camp. It was a most incongruous garment to single out for a possible reunion with one's husband: made of gossamer-thin material, it was dark green with pale pink flowers and a generous number of glittering sequins. I kept it in a brown paper bag, together with a tiny piece of lipstick I had saved for the special occasion and a broken fragment of mirror. How often had I pictured myself, all dolled up, waiting to be taken in John's arms. Never mind my bare feet, my legs with sores, my skeleton body or my tangled hair, I would be beautiful, I would be desirable. How often I used to daydream about it, forgetting the shorts I had fashioned by cutting off the legs of a pair of soldiers' trousers (also found under the house) and the triangular piece of cloth with a drawstring around the neck which covered my flat chest.

Even the fact that postcards occasionally arrived bearing the stamps and postmarks of Thailand, Burma or elsewhere would not budge us from the conviction that our husbands were not far away. We came to the conclusion that these foreign names were the code names for the prisoner of war (POW) camps on Java, designed to confuse us and make us think that the men were far away. How self-deceiving, how short-sighted this attitude seems in hindsight, but it was another support with which to shore up our fragile hopes.

I received three cards from John during the war. They bore the postmark of Burma, they all looked very official, the paper was of poor quality, but to me they were worth their weight in gold. They were of a standard printed content, but the POW had to fill in blanks that had been left; for instance, the POW could choose 'good' or 'excellent' as a description of his condition and he could fill in the amount of pocket money he earned. I recognised John's handwriting and he identified himself by mentioning my name and those of the children. Receiving these cards were unforgettable moments because they were proof that he was still alive recently. We women compared our cards and shook our heads about the childishness of the Japanese to go to such lengths to try to convince us that our husbands had been shipped to foreign countries.

Every time we had received a card, we were allowed to send one back (just ordinary postcards) and of course we used the address that had been on the one that had just arrived. We had a length limit of ten words and we tried to cram into these few words as much valuable information as possible. Once I was so lucky to be able to make use of the card of another person who had nobody to write to. I printed the message on one card and drew a picture of the four children in profile on the other one. After the war I found out that John had received all the cards. The one with the picture arrived at a crucial time. John had been suffering from repeated attacks of dysentery and malaria, and the last malaria bout had affected him so badly that he was considered to have come to the end of the road. He was vaguely aware that his bamboo stretcher had been placed apart in a corner, when suddenly Paddy, a little, red-haired Australian mate of his, appeared next to his bed and bent over him, showing him the card. It pulled him back from semi-consciousness and was the encouragement he needed to help him fight for his life.

69

Towards the end of 1944 we were confronted with the decision of the Japanese overlords to move the inmates of our camp to another city. Different names were whispered: Semarang (in Middle Java), Jakarta, and even Surabaya in East Java. It was Jakarta.

A nervous, restless feeling crept over the community. It was as if an ant colony were being disturbed. After two years in the same place, going from bad to worse, we had become numbed in our miserable existence, we had more or less holed ourselves in. We had found relative security surrounded by friends and familiar landmarks such as a tree, the house, the street. Our world had shrunk to our immediate environs within a perimeter that could be walked around in twenty minutes. A miniature world indeed, but with physical and mental resistance so low, any disturbance brought emotional fluttering and fearful anticipation. What is awaiting us? Where will we go? What will the conditions be like? Will we lose our friends?

Again we had to pack our belongings, but this time the luggage we were allowed to take was greatly reduced and of course we had to leave all the furniture behind, in my case the old wardrobe, the little desk, the low round table, the study lamp. Nelleke's cot had to stay too, but we were assured that mattresses would be provided in the new place.

To our great relief and joy Mart and I found

that our names were on the same list for one of the camps—so were Georgette's and her daughter's. But we had to say goodbye to Karsia, my sister-in-law, and her children who were going to a camp just outside Jakarta. I would not see them again until a few weeks after the peace was signed in August 1945.

My memory is hazy about the last few days of our stay in Kareës, about the packing, the farewell to friends and family, the transport from camp to railway station. At the station we were packed into waiting trains bound for Tjideng camp, a name that still sends a chill along my spine. For many it was their last trip.

CHAPTER SEVEN

The carriages of the long train that took us to Jakarta were old and extremely dirty and the Japanese guards packed as many of us as possible into them. The windows were all boarded up so we could not look out. There were no toilet facilities and the open doors at the end were easily guarded to make escape impossible. After we were loaded on, our carriages were shunted on to a siding where we remained several hours. The heat inside became almost unbearable and the stench of sweating bodies, urine and excrement was overwhelming.

The children were limp with fatigue and exhaustion. I rationed the water in the bottle strapped around my waist, as I did not know how long the wait and the trip itself would take. I also had some cold boiled rice in a tin that I had kept from the day before, but the children did not seem very hungry. I took a handful myself as I knew I had to keep my strength up for what lay ahead. I made the four children as comfortable as possible on the two seats allocated to us and crawled under the seats on the floor to stretch out my long frame. It was not pleasant down there, what with the vomit around me and the smell of urine.

Towards late afternoon, when it started to cool off a bit, there were sounds of loud shouting, banging on the sides of carriages and whistles. At last the long train began to move, at first slowly, with some stopping and starting, but then it got up quite a speed. A welcome breeze flowed through the carriage. Every so often the train stopped for no obvious reason and then with great effort started to choof-choof uphill. It had to tackle some mountainous country before eventually and gradually descending into the coastal lowlands.

The children became brighter as soon as we started to move and the temperature dropped considerably. I crawled out from under the seat and took Peter and Nelleke on my lap while Johnny and Manya tried to peer through some slits between the boards over the windows. All four were excited to be in a train that moved, puffing along at such speed and whistling and rattling through the tunnels. Once we were in the lower country and still a long way from our destination, the train slowly came to a halt at a railway station where there was much shouting. We stopped for such a long time that we thought we must have been going to spend the night there.

By now it was pitch dark and no lamps were lit in the carriages. The only light came from the railway station through the carriage doors and the cracks between the boards. After drinking greedily their meagre ration from the water-bottle and eating their share of the rice, the children fell into a fitful sleep, the two little ones on my lap, the older ones leaning against me.

Despair was taking hold of the carriage again. The long wait was something very few could cope with after such an exhausting day, children were whimpering and some were crying loudly, when a woman not far from me started to sing. A few more joined in and their voices sounded strong and clear as they sang hymns and some well-known national songs. A Japanese guard banged his stick against the carriage, trying to silence them. I heard him ask someone in a guttural voice in Indonesian what and why these women were singing and the answer came in the Indonesian singsong tone: 'Because they are mad.'

I tried to sing with them but couldn't. The tears streamed down my face as I held my children tightly to me. I was immensely proud of these women who kept up the faltering morale with their strong voices. Never before had these simple songs sounded so beautiful and inspiring to me.

At long last the train started to move again and without further stopping we arrived late that night in Jakarta. We were loaded into open trucks, standing up and packed tightly together, and our luggage was thrown in amongst us. A bag hit Manya on the shoulder and I remember how she cried and how I tried to console her. It was bedlam, and there was much shouting and pushing. Finally the trucks started to move off with their pitiful loads.

At the entrance gate to Tjideng the trucks stopped and with difficulty we all got down and retrieved our meagre possessions. A wide road led to an open space, a sort of parade ground, and along this road the sorry procession started to move. Most of us stumbled more than walked, dead-tired, hungry and thirsty, while impatient Japanese guards, with angry words and an occasional strike with their sticks, urged us to hurry up.

Nelleke was slumped over my shoulder and in my free hand I carried the suitcase with our few precious belongings. The other children hung on to me and clutched each other's hands. Inhabitants of the camp lined the wide street on both sides. By the light of the few dim streetlamps I saw their haggard, frightened faces and almost collapsed. I felt I could not go on. From those all around me I heard exclamations of despair and children crying. I called out to the silent, passive onlookers: 'Please help. Can't you see we cannot go on?' Urgent whispers came in answer: 'We can't do anything. We are so sorry. We would be punished.' It was like a nightmare, it didn't seem real, and I saw then that the camp we had left that morning was a picnic ground in comparison. Only that morning? It seemed a lifetime had elapsed since then.

We made it to the 'parade ground', but just. Flopping down on the cool earth, all we wanted to do was close our eyes, fall asleep and forget where we were. But waiting for us were cooked vegetables in big pots and containers of rice and, realising how hungry we were, we wolfed down the food. Tin plates were distributed by concerned, motherly women from the central kitchen who had prepared the meal for us latecomers. There was hot tea as well and for each cup there was rationed one precious spoonful of sugar. No milk, of course—we had not seen any of that for over a year now.

The food and drink gave us renewed energy. When the meal was finished we were ordered to form rows of about twenty people, one behind the other. People covered the entire parade ground, as the already established inmates had also been summoned to take part in the ceremony. The lights were turned up higher and on a raised platform appeared a Japanese in uniform. It was the camp commander, the notorious Sonei. We heard later that he was already infamous for his cruel treatment of POWs in Singapore. He had been recently transferred to this women's camp, a degradation for a man who already had an inferiority complex through being declared medically unfit to fight as a soldier at the front. He was literally a lunatic—I still remember with great apprehension the time around full moon when he would rage and rant around the camp, kicking or maiming anybody who did not immediately obey him or who provoked his displeasure.

Sonei commanded silence and through his interpreter laid down the camp's strict rules. Total obedience was required and absolute adherence to the law as he proclaimed it. We had to work hard, he said, and we would soon realise that this was not as comfortable or easygoing as the place we had come from, where we had been spoilt rotten. When he left the platform with his two bodyguards, we were at last allowed to go to the rooms allocated to us. Tjideng was a very large camp and already thousands of women and children had been living here for quite some time. The accommodation was much poorer than in Kareës, as many more people were cramped into each house.

The friendly street-leader showed us our rooms, and luckily Mart's room was in the same house, two doors down the passageway. My room was incredibly small and could just contain the two old mattresses that covered the floor. Mart was sharing her room, also rather small, with another mother and her child. I remember only that we just dropped down on the mattresses. With a clean rag I washed the faces and hands of the children who by then were almost unconscious from exhaustion; they fell fast asleep before I finished towelling them dry. I had pushed the mattresses together so that we had a large enough area to stretch ourselves out on. Just as I was making myself as comfortable as possible I heard a loud bell sounding in the street outside the house and a voice through a loud-hailer barking out some orders. I did not know what was going on but I heard footsteps coming through the hall and the street-leader calling out to all newcomers to assemble at the parade ground. She poked her head around the door and said to me: 'Come quickly, please hurry.'

I was astonished and almost speechless with anger. I said: 'I am sorry, but we are not coming. Can't you see that these children are so tired? I won't wake them up.' She pleaded with me: 'Please, don't do that to us, we all have to suffer, we all will be punished.' And I asked: 'But why, we have just been there?' And she answered: 'Sonei wants you to know from the start what a strict camp this is. Please, come.' And off she went to the other rooms and to the next house.

I looked at the sleeping children by the light of the small bulb hanging from the ceiling. I saw how pale they looked, how emaciated, with dark shadows under their eyes. I shook them gently. One by one they woke up and looked around, not recognising where they were. Closing their eyes they flopped down again, no energy left to face the world. But I persisted and gradually I got them all up on their feet, and tried to explain why I had to do this cruel thing to them. I took Nelleke over my shoulder, held Peter by the hand and Manya and Johnny held on to me while we tried to make our way through the few badly lit streets to the parade ground. Mart and her little Maryke were close behind. Again we were pushed and shoved into rows of twenty. We were counted over and over again and then, as in bad theatre, Sonei reappeared on the platform, strutted around pompously, and repeated his speech about order and strictness and punishment.

At last we were allowed to return to our rooms and, without further ado, made our way back. Carefully I laid Nelleke down on the bedding. She had fallen asleep on my shoulder and the other children flopped down, falling asleep before they hit the mattress. A commotion erupted outside and women congregated on the footpath. Some of them were crying and some covered their faces with their hands in a mute gesture of despair. I heard what happened. When we were all leaving the parade ground, one little boy, aged almost four, had managed to wriggle free from his mother's hand to explore the little stall where our food and drink had been distributed a few hours before. He tried to climb on to the counter but missed his step and fell into a half-full drum of tea which was still hot. Bystanders quickly pulled him out and he was taken to the camp hospital with burns over most of his body. He was not expected to live. He was one of Peter's lively playmates from Kareës.

His mother and three older sisters had been allocated a room one street away from me, and after asking Mart to keep an eye on my sleeping youngsters, I hurried to their house, which was identified for me, anxiously watching out for guard patrols and hiding behind a wall or the corner of a house, as it was by now of course well past the curfew hour. I found the mother with the girls in their room, and their neighbours were there to comfort them. She had just come back from the hospital where the little boy had died

without regaining consciousness. I put my arms around her, wordlessly, and she clung for a moment to me, then composed herself, and held her daughters in an embrace. There were no tears for such grief, she was evidently in shock, but fully aware of what had happened. Her faith in a God who was wise beyond human comprehension sustained her there and then and kept her sane for the sake of her three distraught daughters and the husband she was convinced she would meet again after the war. I could find no words for the deep admiration I felt for this strong woman—I could only offer her my love.

Years later, I met up with her again and met her husband. The girls had grown up beautifully, and there was also a blond, blue-eyed son, conceived immediately after their emotional reunion, the spitting image of the boy I remembered from Kareës.

The next morning in Tjideng we were woken up early by the same gloomy bell we had heard the night before. It called us once more to the parade ground, a procedure that was repeated every morning and every night at six o'clock. Each time we had to assemble in our rows and be counted, a process that was called *tenko*. It was often a very trying thing, as it might be a very long time before the Japanese who were in charge of the counting were satisfied and the numbers tallied. Matters were complicated for worried mothers when a child urgently had to go to the toilet, as nobody was allowed to leave the grounds until the end. If you were standing towards the end of a row, it was not too difficult to let the child do what was necessary because from the front, where the Japanese stood, it was not easy to see what happened right at the back. Mothers with small children tried to squeeze in at the end of rows and the others usually co-operated. Sometimes, when a child was standing in the front half of the row, he or she would be secretively handed over from one to the other towards the back and afterwards handed back.

After *tenko* in the morning we lined up with our bowls for breakfast, a few liquid spoonfuls of tapioca cooked in water. We had not eaten bread since the first year in Kareës and sometimes had hallucinations of crisp, fresh bread covered generously with golden butter, something else not seen for the last eighteen months or so. No eggs, cheese or other dairy products came into the camp, and fruit and practically all vegetables—in particular raw salad vegetables—appeared only in our dreams. Besides the bowl of watery gruel in the morning, the only other food for the day was a cup of boiled rice with some vegetables for lunch and again for the evening meal. The vegetables were generally a sort of Indonesian spinach called *kang-kung* and onions boiled in water.

How we craved for some sweet dish, some creamed rice with sugar, or custard or apple sauce! It was especially hard on the children. I wished I could spoil them with some easily digestible, sweet-tasting morsels, light and colourful, and in my dreams I fed them strawberries and cream. It was an amazing phenomenon that, being completely deprived of tasty, nourishing, appetising food, we were crazy about the recipe pages in old magazines. We collected them, exchanged them, discussed the finer points of cooking, and drooled over colourful photos of tempting dishes. Strange as it may sound, this culinary voyeurism gave us a certain satisfaction: it made us aware that beautiful food still existed, somewhere, and that we had been able to enjoy it too before the war. And we were convinced that one day—please God make it soon—we would be able to indulge ourselves again.

I remember that I was continuously so ravenously hungry that sometimes I did not know what to do. I invented a means that temporarily relieved the gnawing feeling by touching with a moist finger a mixture of salt and pepper in the lid of a cigarette tin, and delicately licking the finger clean. During the first months in Kareës I had developed a stomach complaint which prevented food from being digested properly. It passed through the body in record time, so that I did not benefit much from the already vitamin- and mineral-deficient diet. I have a large frame and always had a very good appetite, so that from the beginning the condition caused me a great problem. During the first year, when the quantity and even the quality of our food seemed sufficient to stay alive, I was already having to fight the constant nagging feeling of an empty stomach.

Everyone who came to the communal kitchen to be 'dished up' received the same quantity in the outstretched bowl, so that the children fortunately, received in comparison a better deal than the adults. Even so, the ration did not contain any of the ingredients vital for growing children, and I often worried about what the lack of balance in the diet would do to them. But there was nothing I could do about it—and I had to eat my own portion, I had to finish it, because I was the one who had to keep going, for the children's sake.

The mortality rate in the camp became frighteningly high and children especially fell victim to a number of diseases. Whooping cough, an ugly and debilitating sickness, was rampant in Tjideng when we arrived. Vaccination against it was unheard of in those days and there was practically no remedy for it. In the overcrowded conditions the weak, starving children were entirely at risk.

My children seemed to withstand the onslaught of the nasty, choking cough for quite a while, but eventually all four succumbed. It was terrifying to hear the bouts of sustained coughing which seemed to tear their lungs apart and left them exhausted. Each had an empty milk-tin handy to receive the coughed-up phlegm after the nerve-racking attack had subsided. The illness was worse at night, and one after the other the children would be woken up by the noise of the first to feel the dreaded attack coming on. In the half-darkness—lights were not allowed between 10 p.m. and 6 a.m.—it was difficult to comfort them all at once. When at last their lungs were clear of the irritating mucus they would fall asleep again and, with a sigh of relief, so would I. Until the next attack. This went on for several months.

It was a miracle that they all survived. As well as whooping cough, they also suffered from amoebic and bacillary dysentery, malaria, and the greatest killer, starvation. How often during the night I groped for a limp arm or felt a feverish forehead and prayed for strength and faith. And in the morning when I awoke to see them alive and breathing, I thanked God that we made it to another day.

CHAPTER EIGHT

One of our biggest problems in Tjideng was sanitation. The toilets frequently became blocked when the septic tanks filled up. Drastic solutions were needed to get rid of the toxic waste from the camp and the Japanese devised an indescribably sordid means. We had to dig a canal about eighty centimetres wide and just as deep and, with buckets and long-handled scoops, empty the contents of the tanks into it. Straddling the canal at short intervals women with hessian mats fastened on to sticks had to move the foul-smelling brown mass along, towards the high fence on the camp perimeter. The canal passed under the fence to a sort of receiving depot, most probably a very large, deep pit which must have been a source of many fatal infections for the local population.

There was a guard with a rifle at the temporary breach in the fence to prevent the unlikely escape of anyone desperate enough to try to float out in the sewer. To my knowledge no one ever did.

Everyone had to work in the 'cleaning gangs' on weekly shifts. To make matters worse, there was practically no water in which to clean up afterwards. Soap of course was a luxury we had not seen for a long time; salt was used instead, be it for washing hands, utensils or clothes. For a period towards the end of our stay, each person received only one cup of water a day—for drinking, bathing and washing. This was not even enough to satisfy our thirst, so we went around permanently dirty.

Deadly diseases such as hepatitis and bacillary dysentery were rife and scores of women and children died every day. Death was a constant companion always there in the shadows. The possibility of survival looked grim.

You lived each day as it came, from mealtime to mealtime, hoping that once in a while something extra would be dished up. Twice a week we received a few pieces of *tempe*, compressed, dried, fermented soyabeans cut into thin slices and fried. Besides being delicious, they were actually life-saving. Quite a few people died when the *tempe* was withdrawn for two weeks in punishment for somebody's alleged disobedience. Whenever a person did the wrong thing, even if unwittingly, the whole camp was made to suffer. Our anxiety about this was almost tangible. Nobody ventured into the streets unnecessarily for fear of encountering Sonei or one of his henchmen looking for a scapegoat.

On two occasions we had to go the whole day without food. The street-leaders came to every house and urged us to use as little energy as possible; we tried to get the children to lie down for long periods to conserve their strength. But in spite of the special efforts we all made, the enforced fast caused many deaths.

Towards evening one day truckloads of offal arrived in the camp, with orders that the horrible mess was to be distributed to all the houses. The street-leaders worked frantically to deposit the already foul-smelling intestines, hearts, tails and genitals on the ground in backyards, where they were a macabre sight in the torchlight. Perhaps it was meant as a sick joke—we had no way of cooking it—but such was our hunger that the thought of meat of whatever kind was so tempting that each woman gratefully accepted her portion of the weird-looking 'extra' and took it to her living area.

We had to put lids on the containers and weigh them down with stones because that night the rats were attracted by the strong smell. Some rats even managed to remove the lids. In any case there was a lot of noise, clanging of metal and squeaking, and once I felt a rat running over my face. I screamed and pulled the children to me and put my arms around them—they were greatly disturbed by all the commotion. By that stage we were no longer occupying the small room (we had had to make room for another family) and our two mattresses were now in a corner of the dining room. As this opened on to the garden, the rats had easy access to our area. There were now so many women and children in the camp that there was not a patch of floor space left.

The next morning our attempts to start a fire between two stones in the garden were futile, so we finished up taking the putrid gift of the Japanese administration to the kitchens to be destroyed; perhaps it still found its way to us disguised in the vegetable soup.

When the war was over I read a few books describing the experiences and hardships of life under an oppressive invader. One well-known account, *Woman in Berlin*, told of a grisly incident in which an emaciated horse, drawing a cart, collapsed in the street whereupon women came from all directions and started cutting pieces of flesh from the still-breathing animal. It sickened me to read about that; from my experience I knew that such behaviour was not typical of starving people. A stray cat for example would have been welcomed as a pet, a substitute for those most of us had to leave behind. But they were scrawny and wild and disappeared under the fence as soon as they were approached. I remember thinking how it would have been had we had a dog with us in the worst months of our starvation: we would have put our arms around each other and the dog and would have faced the end that way. We were so lacking in energy that we would not have been able to be aggressive, nor could we have carried on sexual relations. I realised this when the children and I had moved to a hospital camp where we could mix with male prisoners. They were in a similar state of exhaustion.

Thank God, nature accommodated itself to our changed mental and physical states. For most women and girls their menstrual period stopped after a few months of imprisonment, mercifully so, as any loss of blood would have hastened the physical decline. Moreover, the unhygienic conditions and the lack of water would have added to the discomfort and despair. It was amazing how soon their periods returned once the war ended, the prison gates opened, and an abundance of food arrived in the camps for distribution. But that moment was still several months and many agonising experiences away.

Mart and little Maryke were still surviving against all odds, and so were we. The bond between us became even stronger, if that were possible. We had our meals together, and as we sat on our mattresses, or on the floor if there was space available, our eyes frequently met over the heads of our children with the unspoken question: How long can we last? Mart was unselfishness personified. On one occasion she pushed her plate with some rice left on it towards me with the words: 'Would you, please, finish that. I couldn't eat any more.' I knew it was a lie and I hated myself when I gulped down the extra spoonful. I can still remember the look of gentle satisfaction on her face. She always maintained that she was a small eater due to her slim build, and she appreciated that I needed more calories just to survive.

Years later I discussed with a friend the fact that my children had grown up in the shadow of imprisonment, sickness, starvation and death, and in the absence of social graces. It was a miracle that they were not scarred for life, in one way or another. I come from a very strong family from which I inherited physical toughness and an ability to recuperate against the odds. But what mental and emotional damage the children could have suffered from those long years of deprivation of all that was light and happy and beautiful.

They grew up mentally and emotionally balanced, with far above average intelligence and no trace of bitterness or resentment. They became healthy fathers and mothers, and when I look at them and at their lovely children I feel as if the story I am writing is from a totally different life, far removed from the present.

When I questioned my friend, an educationist, about the apparent absence of trauma in my children's lives, she said: 'Don't forget, they always had you, day and night. You slept with your arms around them and during the day they could never stray far from you. You were their security amidst uncertainty, terror and death. Many of the children of our affluent society grow up insecure and unloved, provided with all the material welfare money can buy but lacking the basic comfort of parental love and care.' Parental love and care was what all the children needed more than anything during the hellish days in Tjideng.

They always found something to play with and we often marvelled at their ingenuity in coming up with new games. Lack of energy prevented the rougher type of play among youngsters as they were often listless or had to lie down after strenuous activity. Every day another little friend gave up the struggle to stay alive; they were carried out through the camp gates in a simple coffin, leaving behind one more distraught mother to cope with her grief.

Sometimes I searched the camp for some greenery or a single flower, but thousands of feet had trampled the ground and there was not one blade of grass left, not even along the fences. The earth was brown and hard but a downpour turned the camp into one big mudpool. How we enjoyed those sporadic rains! They gave us fresh water and we danced and sang as the showers came down. Of course, the mosquitoes thrived in the pools of water that remained, so the blessing was accompanied by renewed attacks of malaria.

One day I suddenly felt very strange and almost fainted, something that had never happened to me before. My heart started to palpitate, my pulse raced and became weak and I do not remember much about what happened after that. When I came to I was in a bed in the small overcrowded hospital on the outskirts of the camp. Mart was there to persuade me that this was the best solution for me: after complete rest for a few days I would be as good as new. She would look after my children with the help of a young woman, Eva, who had entered Kareës with us and was devoted to the children. There was no medicine available to treat whatever had struck me—which was a mild heart attack— and the nurses hoped that with the prescribed rest I would stand a chance of being on my feet again in a few days.

It was difficult having to be away from the children, although Mart brought them in to see me, but it was luxurious to lie on a softer bed than usual and to feel the gentle hands and loving care of the nurses. There was none of that feeling of being constantly on the go and there was no communal work—just rest, absolute rest. It must have done the trick. After a few days, when an opportunity arose for me and the children to leave the death camp and go to the St Vincentius hospital camp, I was more than ready to take up the challenge. It appeared that St Vincentius had been a Catholic boarding school, about half an hour's drive from Tjideng in the small town of Djatinegara, which was more or less an outlying suburb of greater Jakarta. It was a large, modern building with extensive grounds and seemed marvellously suited to a hospital camp, the classrooms easily converting to wards. The plan to make the boarding school a prisoners' hospital was new and the Japanese administration was looking for able-bodied women to provide the nursing and work as kitchen and general cleaning staff. Tjideng had to provide a contingent of strong, preferably unmarried women. Eva was selected; she asked if she could bring her 'family' with her, meaning mine, omitting to mention that there were four young children.

Everything happened very quickly. Most women tried to leave Tjideng and in the confusion I slipped out of my hospital bed, packed our simple belongings and boarded the trucks waiting to take us to Djatinegara.

Mart stayed behind with Maryke, as young children were forbidden to go. I knew the risk I was taking, but felt I had to take it. Every decision to make a change was a plunge into the unknown: it might mean death or else a temporary reprieve. Mart and I clung to each other and wept, she assuring me that this was my only chance. I knew too that if I stayed in Tjideng I would not live much longer. And I had to stay alive at all costs, to be with my children and, with God's help, to steer them through to freedom.

CHAPTER NINE

As we drove along the road from Tjideng, packed into open trucks like sardines, we looked for the first time in more than two years at the world outside a prison camp. It seemed strange that life had been going on as usual; people still lived in their humble stone and bamboo houses, there were small shops and tall, shady trees lined the roads. However, we were shocked at how neglected and drab everything looked, even in the brilliant sunshine. The roads were full of potholes, paintwork was cracked and peeling, whitewashed walls grimy and in need of repair. The people looked under-nourished and their clothes were shabby.

Children ran along some distance with the trucks, laughing and clowning as children do, but the older people stood grim-faced and silent; some youths called out obscenities. The small wayside shops and restaurants, formerly always stacked to capacity with fruit and vegetables and miscellaneous wares, were half empty, and sadly missing were the gay colours and brilliant patterns of the women's sarongs and *slendangs* (shawls). The war years had taken their toll on the population; and besides the poverty there was the overriding fear and anxiety.

The Japanese guards on the trucks were not unduly harsh. They seemed to view the trip as a sort of holiday outing and joked with each other. Even they had probably not been out of the camp for quite a while.

When we arrived in St Vincentius we were surprised at the good condition of the buildings, the beauty of the church near the entrance and the attractiveness of the buildings leading away from it on both sides. The front garden looked well kept and tall trees provided shade. And flowers—incredible, I thought I was dreaming—brilliant red and yellow cannas. And the fresh country air, how we had missed that during the last few years!

The large doors of the empty church stood wide open and we were ushered in, one small group at a time, until the trucks were empty and the nave practically filled up. I cannot say for sure how many of us there were, but I would guess about sixty. I saw how many children there were, some mothers had four or five gathered around them and I tried to hide myself in the corner furthest away with Nelleke on my arm and the other three clutching on to Eva and me. Now and then a whooping-cough attack threatened their poor, wheezing lungs and I begged them to stifle it as much as possible. They were still in the last weeks of the sickness, but the attacks were now neither so severe nor so frequent.

The Japanese commander of the hospital stood on a sort of dais in the place where the altar must once have been and next to him stood a woman, the interpreter. The man's name was Dr Mizukuchi. He was youngish-looking and in uniform, but his manner was not at all that of a soldier and his voice was rather soft. We heard later that he had done his medical studies in Germany, so the German language must have been quite familiar to him. Although most of us would have been able to understand had he spoken German, he considered it an insult to us to do so as Holland had fallen to Germany at that time.

The interpreter was the daughter of an American man and a Japanese woman and she was married to a Dutch man who was a POW somewhere on Java. Being half Japanese she could have stayed out of the camp but she had chosen to share the fate of the Dutch women. With her knowledge of all three languages, she was an ideal interpreter. All of these were particulars that we heard later, but they were indicative of the personalities as we encountered them on that first day.

I thought I was dreaming—the contrast with the camp we had just left was astounding. I looked up into the vault of the church and my eyes feasted on the beauty. Through the open side door I could see a peaceful courtyard. And the two gentle-looking people preparing to talk to the newcomers were too good to be true. Was there indeed life after Sonei? It seemed heaven to me and inwardly I sent up a prayer of thanks.

Mrs Bakker, the interpreter, started to tell us in Dutch that we were now in a hospital camp and that we were expected to work hard. The first lot of patients had arrived in the last few days, some nurses were attending to them, and kitchen and cleaning staff were flat out trying to cope with the work. We were most welcome and should start work as soon as we were sorted out.

First the single women and mothers with one or two older children were called forward and shown to their sleeping quarters. Several families remained standing in separate groups, anxiously awaiting their fates. Eva had gone with the single women and I tried to make my group look as small as possible, holding Nelleke tight and urging the children to stand very close to me. As we were waiting Mizukuchi and Mrs Bakker slowly walked up to the largest group, a mother with five children of whom the eldest looked about ten. They explained to her that they could not stay in St Vincentius but had to go back to Tjideng, as it was impossible to have too many children on the premises. The mother was most distressed, but a few years of camp life had taught her that arguing and protesting were fruitless. With her young family she retreated to the trucks still waiting outside.

Dr Mizukuchi proceeded to the next group and Mrs Bakker repeated her fateful message. Cold sweat broke out all over me, my heart started to beat faster and I felt I was going to faint. With a great effort I managed to stand my ground and prayed silently: Dear God, please, not this. The children felt the anxiety too and my trembling hands must have conveyed my fear as one after the other they started to cough, the long drawn-out whoops echoing round the big church. By that time all the other family groups had left and I felt Mizukuchi and his companion walking towards me. When they stopped a few paces away I looked up slowly, waiting for the sentence that would crush us and that most probably I would not survive.

There must have been so much despair in my eyes, that a slow, gentle smile spread over his face and he stretched out his hand and stroked Nelleke's hair. Then he said something in Japanese to Mrs Bakker and walked away. She smiled at me and said: 'Dr Mizukuchi wants you to stay. You don't need to go back to Tjideng.' And she turned and rejoined Mizukuchi who was arranging accommodation for the single women. I could not believe my ears. I sat down on the floor, put my arms around my children, and sobbed my heart out. Their coughing had subsided now and they overwhelmed me with questions: May we stay now? We don't need to go back? Where will we sleep?

I controlled myself and, looking in the direction where Mizukuchi was giving orders through the interpreter, resolutely got to my feet and walked towards him, the children staying close to me. I stopped, respectfully, a few paces away, and asked for Mrs Bakker's attention. She looked at me and I said to her that I wanted to express my gratitude to the doctor. She conveyed my message and, bowing to him, I said: *'Arigato gozaimasu.'* At the same time he bowed to me, quickly, and looked slightly embarrassed. He seemed very young then and his face wore that quizzical air which I often detected later whenever he tried to conceal his shyness.

Mrs Bakker told me that Dr Mizukuchi had decided to give me a good room, away from the other people, because of the illness of my children. I just had to wait a while and she would take me there herself. After all the workers had been shown to their respective dormitories, Mrs Bakker took our little group through the side door, across the courtyard and into a huge room with a high ceiling and marble floor, a sort of ante room of the church. She told me that the courtyard belonged to this room and that I had the exclusive use of it. The children could sit out in the sun, she said, and all that fresh air would soon make them better.

I was overwhelmed. The children started to explore the courtyard, the private little garden. They played with the beautiful white stones and pebbles. How clean everything looked. Then the door into the wide passage which divided our room from the church proper was thrown open and some iron beds and mattresses were brought in, a table and a few stools. We had not seen proper beds for years and the children thought it quite daring to sleep so high. There were pillows too, so comfortable; and the children kept going in and out of the room as if to stake out their claim on the property.

Eva had joined us, as I had told Mrs Bakker that she belonged to us. By then we had to go and join the queues for our midday meal and returned to the room with our bowls filled with the standard fare of watery soup and rice. The quantity was scarcely bigger than we were used to and by then we were so hungry that we gulped it down in record time. Eva had to report for work immediately afterwards, as a ward cleaner, and I lay down for a few moments as I felt that I could not take much more just then. Peter and Nelleke had a nap and John and Manya continued exploring the garden. I realised that, having been accepted in this hospital camp, I was expected to pull my weight in the workforce. I had not breathed a word about my heart complaint or the fact that until this morning I had been confined to a hospital bed. Being promoted from patient to hospital worker in twenty-four hours was not a bad record, but I had to prove my claim that I was an able worker, especially on account of my generous treatment by the camp commander.

The next morning, after *tenko* and the breakfast of thin tapioca gruel, I went to the Dutch office where the woman in charge of the work timetable allotted me the job of cleaning the bathrooms and toilets. I had to do that twice a day and she thought that I could fit it in with my main responsibility of looking after my children. It turned out that the office had appointed a young mother with a six-year-old child to mind the children of women at work. There was a shed in the back garden where they could find shelter from rain or the midday sun and the large lawn was ideal for playing and listening to stories.

I walked around, still half-dazed, and took the children along the path and corridors that connected the many classrooms, now sick wards. Most beds were already occupied and nurses, wearing a sort of rough white apron that distinguished them from the general workers, moved amongst them. As I passed by, there was a sudden flurry of activity as a new batch of patients arrived. One of the wards was for men and I remember how shocked I was when my eyes caught the first glimpse of Dutch men in about two years. A lot of them were very old and they all looked as if they were at death's door. They had come from civilian camps, and only the most seriously ill were admitted. For practically all of the patients the trip to the hospital was to be a journey of no return. There were few medicines available and, as elsewhere, the ultimate killer was starvation.

The 'wards' were very airy and open, so the patients did not have much privacy, but what had they known of that precious feeling for years now? The airiness was a welcome change, at least. In the weeks and months to come the wards were filled to capacity. When they ran out of beds, stretchers hastily made from bamboo, were lined up so close to each other that nurses could hardly move amongst them. The system only worked because the number of crudely made cane and canvas coffins that left by the back door each day somehow matched the number of new admissions.

When I took the children to the field behind the hospital on that first morning after my arrival, the scene was still rather peaceful and to my eyes, seemed incredibly neat and clean and modern. And there was plenty of water, imagine that! And the sun was shining and we were alive, the children tugging at my hands, happy and excited about their new life. I thought of Mart and Maryke, of all my good friends and family, of John—and I prayed in silence: Please, God, help us all.

The field was surprisingly lush, with borders of beautiful flowers, and I breathed deeply the fresh smells of outdoor life I had all but forgotten. How it was possible that this school and the grounds had been kept in such excellent condition during the years was a mystery.

I left the children with the kind young woman who was to mind them and hurried off to start my job. Taking the bucket and scrubbing brush (what luxuries) and a jar of salt, I began to clean the first of the small bathrooms. It contained a big cement basin filled with water, and a small container used for scooping up water and splashing yourself all over, the true Indonesian way. I quickly tired, but finished in good time, and marvelled at the abundance of fresh water. When I went up to clean the row of toilets, a short distance away, my stomach turned over. The patients who could still move around a little were generally too sick to be able to clean themselves properly and it was a big task sluicing away most of the filth before I could start scrubbing. The toilet at the end of the row bore the sign 'Danger—Dysentery' in big red letters, and the adjacent ward was marked likewise. I found out later that nobody came out of this ward alive. The patients were all dangerously ill and, because they were highly infectious, they were isolated in the one large special ward. The nurses spent their time running out to the special toilet with bedpans and rushing back to the next patient who was calling out in agony. The nurses wore crude masks in a pathetic attempt to avoid contamination. The stench that lingered around this toilet and came wafting through the open doors of the dysentery ward was beyond description. It was the smell of death.

I found a bottle of disinfectant and used the special brush to clean the toilet and the spattered walls and floor as best as I could. Then I disinfected my hands and arms and legs and went quickly to one of the bathrooms and splashed myself with water. What admiration I had for the nurses in general, and especially for those working in that particular ward. Now I could understand why single women were preferred in the hospital: it was no place for children and I had to keep mine as far as possible away from that dangerous area of the building.

When I arrived back in my room I lay down for a moment, having never felt so weak as during these days since the heart attack. I did my cleaning round three more times and thought I was going to faint on the last occasion. After I recovered, I went to the office and told the woman there about my condition. She told me off for not letting her know before and she agreed that the job was really above my capacity. She said that she would look into the possibility of easier work for me and would let me know the next morning. I washed myself in lots of water, went back to my room and collapsed on the bed until the children returned.

CHAPTER TEN

The next morning I found that my new job was one which I could never have imagined in my wildest dreams. I was going to be the wreathmaker. I could not believe my luck. Imagine going into the gardens, picking flowers, cutting small branches and gathering them in a basket!

The woman who had been doing the job since the first death occurred in the hospital a few weeks ago was needed in another part of the hospital. She pointed out to me the hedge that was most suited to provide branches that needed to be strong but easily bent. It was a high, thick hedge with short-stemmed waxy leaves. The flowers would be my own choice. In the small room next to mine she showed me a container with water, a pair of scissors and a thick roll of string. There was also an old wide basket which would hold a mass of greenery and lots of flowers. 'You will need it,' she warned me as she hurried off to her new job. 'Mark my words, you will be a very busy girl.'

Her words were prophetic. Every day new groups of patients arrived, most of them critically ill, some of whom did not even last until evening. As the wards filled up, more nurses were needed, so more women were recruited from Tjideng and other camps. No more children arrived with them and the total number of youngsters remained at about fifteen. I kept an eye out for any women I knew among the new workers, but there were none.

One day, however, as I was putting a jar of flowers on the windowsill outside one ward, I looked in surprise and then with delight at a young woman my age lying in the bed next to the window. She was a very good friend of mine whom I had not seen for a few years; we had known each other since we were twelve. She was not thin as most other women were, but swollen with oedema, which gave her none the less a healthier look.

I quickly went inside and took her hands in mine, and told her how happy I was to see her. She shook her head and searched my face and said: 'But who are you?' I thought her mind must have been wandering, and I said gently to her: 'I am Nell, don't you remember?' At that she broke out in sobs, and we held each other. Then she looked me in the eyes for a long while and said: 'Do you know, I only recognise you now because of your eyes. I have never seen you so thin and so dark.' And she started to cry again. I knew that I had become as brown as a native Indonesian and that my skin had shrunk around my face and limbs and body.

Often I dropped by that window and refilled the jar with fresh flowers. The amazing thing was that my friend, who had been a frail person all her life, survived the prison camp. I met her again in Holland several years later, but she was still very sick when I saw her for the last time before we finally migrated to Australia in 1951.

The number of female patients far outweighed the number of males. Of course we tried to get as much information from the men as possible, and some women even found out where their husbands were. Others had their worst fears confirmed. No military prisoners were admitted at any time, but I remained firmly convinced that John was alive in some camp on Java.

I was continually overawed by the atmosphere in St Vincentius. We could breathe more freely not only because of the clean country air, but also because the fear and oppression we had suffered in Tjideng had been relieved to a large degree. We knew we had Dr Mizukuchi to thank for that. He was medical commander and under him served the

Dutch doctor directly responsible to him for all treatment and decisions regarding patients. There was very little medication available, and Mizukuchi was bound hand and foot by what the Japanese military administration allocated to the hospital. He was the silent force behind everything, always trying to overturn harsh decisions and often getting into strife because of his more humane approach to problems in the camp.

I did not understand the situation enough to know who effectively was in charge. Quite a few uniformed Japanese worked in a separate office, while a few walked around, surveying the scene. There was also a small office where the Dutch doctor resided together with a number of women who were constantly busy with administration, including registering the patients. Mizukuchi had his quarters in a separate part of the building, but we saw him every day conferring with the Dutch doctor as they walked along the corridors accompanied by Mrs Bakker. Sometimes visitors came who appeared to be high Japanese officials on a tour of inspection.

One day when I was sitting on the floor in my flower room, busy bending branches into the required circular shape, Mizukuchi suddenly stood at the open door. He bowed slightly in my direction and bent down to show his companion the wreaths I had already finished. They were lying on the floor, the

pastel shades of the flowers glowing amidst the green of the leaves. The visitor seemed rather impressed and nodded to me; Mizukuchi smiled and was clearly pleased with my work. Wreath making was a full-time job and generally I had to make six or eight a day. The Japanese ordered their wreaths from a florist in town (I wondered if they paid for them). They provided one wreath for each coffin and the Dutch office did likewise, which was where I came in.

Each day in the late afternoon a funeral service was conducted on the back lawn. All the coffins were placed neatly alongside each other, the Dutch floral tributes distributed over the clumsy containers, while a clergyman said a few simple words and prayed. Then Mizukuchi came and laid the other, professional, wreaths and saluted. A loud horn announced the arrival of the 'funeral bus', a big black enclosed truck. It parked alongside the hospital and when the service came to an end, it backed up the path to collect the coffins. They were loaded into the back, the doors were shut and slowly the vehicle with its tragic load drove off through the garden towards the big gates of the front entrance.

There were always some women working along the path, weeding among the flowers or the few vegetables they had planted. As the truck approached they would stop work and straighten up, holding on to rakes and spades.

If they were not fast enough in bowing towards the cortege, the Japanese guards supervising them would strike them for not honouring their dead. The Japanese had an awed respect for death—they themselves bowed reverently although it was they who had been instrumental in filling the coffins in the first place.

I rarely saw Mizukuchi. Whenever we passed him along the corridors, he would give us one of his enigmatic smiles or sometimes stop for a moment and pat one of the children on the head. In the beginning I had been a little apprehensive, feeling that some favour might be expected of me in return for his generous treatment. But his behaviour was always courteous and correct—as if, from a distance, he kept a watchful eye on me. He showed his pleasure when after a few weeks the children finally stopped their loud and penetrating coughing that disturbed the quiet of the night.

Although he tried in many open and many subtle ways to lighten our burdens, he apparently had no say over the food rations and our starvation meals were barely enough to keep us alive. There was always hunger to contend with. When we ate our meals we forced ourselves to eat slowly, to chew every mouthful as if it were our last. One day some grains of boiled rice fell between the bowls of two of the children. They looked at each other and then one said: 'It is yours', and pushed it to the other; the other pushed the precious grains back and said: 'No, it is yours'.

On another day, some bananas suddenly became available but we had not one cent to buy them. Then Peter came into the room, flushed with excitement and clutching one marvellously large golden banana in his arms. A kind lady who still had some hidden coins had given him one of her bananas. Peter put the miracle fruit on the table, while we stood around and watched spellbound. He peeled it solemnly and with concentration, his tongue protruding slightly between his lips, and cut the fruit into six equal parts. He gave us each a piece. It was the sweetest, loveliest banana we had ever tasted.

I sometimes surveyed my wasting body. My breasts had disappeared, my ribs stuck out and my pelvic bones showed clearly through my shorts. During *tenko* one morning Manya wanted to lean against me, but she called out 'Ouch, your bones hurt me.' I sighed, hoping that I would have put on a little bit of weight by the time John took me in his arms.

One day I found some rotten vegetables and half a loaf of bread, green with mould, in the corner of the back garden. They had been thrown out by the Indonesian guards who had their special quarters adjacent to the garden. They were staffing the lookout posts, placed at intervals along the perimeter. I made a fire

113

between two stones (how I did that eludes me now) and in an old tin cooked up a weird-looking porridge of bread and vegetables. The children licked their fingers after the treat.

Quite in contrast to our emaciated bodies, and also the lean figures of the Japanese, there was one Japanese military man who stood out. Sergeant Fukue had a huge belly and was bursting out of his uniform. He also had a big belly laugh which he often alternated with angry shouts and what were obviously curses. He had a little monkey which the children had great fun playing with until its master had enough of that and chased the children away, roughly pulling the monkey back by its lead. Fukue was known to have hit a few old men who could hardly walk for not bowing quickly enough for his liking. He was feared, and sometimes secretly ridiculed.

You did not know what to expect from him from one moment to the other. Sometimes he would barge into my room in the evening and look around suspiciously, most probably to see if I had a male visitor, as once through my open door he had seen a man sitting at my table. This was the husband of a woman I had met in Tjideng; he was seriously ill and could hardly walk and he was very grateful for the information I could give him about his wife. He died a short time later. The other side of Fukue's character was revealed to me one morning when I opened my door into the

114

passage and found a bunch of bananas on the doorstep. I could just see part of a fat leg bound in khaki puttees and ending in a military boot disappearing around the corner. I had my suspicions and when I asked Mrs Bakker if she knew who the generous mystery man was, she said: 'Yes, you are right. It is Fukue. But, please, don't thank him. He doesn't want to know about it. He might fly into a rage.'

On another morning there was a luscious papaya waiting for us, and once—would you believe—a bottle of milk. As I watched the children relishing these unexpected and delicious gifts, I could not help thinking how complicated and contradictory some of God's creatures are. Fukue would grin at my children but when they approached him with shy smiles, obviously wanting to show him how grateful they were, he would send them away with a harsh word.

One woman in the office felt she could afford a joke with Fukue now and then, but only of course when he was in a good mood. One day, however, she miscalculated and went a bit too far. He pretended to be exhausted and stretched himself out on a bench just outside her office, which opened up into the corridor. I happened to walk past with a few wreaths on my way to the garden when she spotted me. With a wicked grin on her face she took one of the wreaths and placed it right on top of his protruding stomach. With agility remarkable for such a fat man he was on his feet in a second, ripping the wreath to pieces. He threw it away and, screaming in fury, picked up the bench and threw it across the corridor. A little table followed and was smashed to smithereens. For one breathless moment I thought that he would grab the woman too and send her flying, but he thought better of it and walked away, suddenly calm and trying to make his exit as dignified as possible.

As the days and weeks wore on, more and more people died. In the hot tropical climate bodies had to be removed on the day of death and no later. If it happened that a patient died half an hour before the funeral truck was due to arrive, attendants in the morgue rushed to prepare another coffin, and I worked feverishly to make up one more wreath.

When another death was imminent, a sheet was pinned up around the bed or the stretcher to give the patient some privacy and dignity during the final moments. The children had grown up with death and were quite matter of fact about it. It happened sometimes that, after passing some wards on their way back from 'school' in the garden, they would hurry to look for me in the flower room, telling me in an offhand manner: 'Mum, you better make another wreath, we just saw the nurses put up a sheet.'

One morning as I walked along the corridors I looked through an open window in a women's ward and saw a bed with a sheet around—not an unusual sight in itself, but this bed was turned, as if to enable the dying person to look outside into the open air; the sheet was shielding the patient on three sides from the goings-on in the ward. I stood still and was shocked to recognise a Russian dancer I had met in Kareës a lifetime ago. I remembered thinking she was the most exquisite person I had ever seen, tiny and as light as a feather, her long dark hair flowing around her as she tried to teach some little girls to dance. She was not young then but it was almost impossible to believe that she was in fact nearing sixty. Now she looked ancient, her tiny face a mask in which the big, dark eyes were staring up into the blue sky, her long, straggly hair spread around her. The butterfly had gone on its journey and the nurse came and closed the sheets around the still figure on the bed.

CHAPTER ELEVEN

'Mum, listen to me, I can read,' Manya held up a book to catch my attention, then put it down on the table. With her finger following the letters she slowly spelled out the words that told of the adventures of the Little Brown Bear. I was happily surprised, as I had not realised that the little gathering of children in the garden were being taught by their 'governess', the friendly young woman who had been joined recently by an elderly nun, a kind and quiet soul. Mizukuchi quite clearly had turned a blind eye to the goings-on in the shade of the large banyan tree, as schooling and education for Dutch children had been taboo from the beginning of the Japanese occupation. Johnny, not wanting to be outdone, showed that he could read too and the little ones were quite impressed. Now we could soon take it in turns to read at bedtime. I marvelled at how quickly they learnt this new skill. There were only a few books doing the rounds, as there were not many children, but these were read and re-read from beginning to end. And they also came home with new songs, so their repertoire was extended beyond the few I had taught them. Feeling the last physical energy slowly draining from our bodies, we became possessed of an urgency to hold on to life with both hands. This will to survive at all costs was a thread drawing us all together, the children and me. No words were needed and none could have expressed this close bond.

Apart from continuous gastric upsets, my children, as if by a miracle, did not succumb to further serious illness, and neither did the other children of the working mothers in the hospital camp. As the patients consisted mainly of the critically ill and the very old, practically no children were admitted to the wards. The one exception was the dysentery ward, where quite a few children were admitted on stretchers. Not many days later, covered by a sheet, they were taken to the morgue, a long narrow room close to the dreaded ward. When I knew that one of the wreaths I had to make one day was for a child's coffin, my fingers trembled as I arranged with extra care the white flowers amongst the green leaves. Silently I prayed for strength for the distraught mother suffering in some other camp who would hear perhaps in a few days' time that her child had died.

Although the sun was shining and the flowers smelled sweet, and we knew our circumstances were infinitely better than in Tjideng, we also knew that our time was slowly running out. The feeling that nothing could stop the gradual deterioration of our bodies unless a drastic change occurred sometimes weighed heavily on me, especially as I became more and more stressed by the increased demand for wreaths. In my overworked imagination I sometimes pictured the funeral truck as a huge black monster, waiting impatiently, snorting furiously and pawing the ground, eager to open its wide mouth and gobble up the row of coffins. The screaming

119

horn, so loud and demanding, pursued me in my dreams to the extent that it became an obsession.

One day I had to go to the morgue to count the bodies as there seemed to be a discrepancy between the number of dead and the number of wreaths that were ordered. The original order was for seven wreaths, but the woman who came from the morgue advised me that there were eight bodies and eight coffins. 'See for yourself and count them,' she said. So I went into the long, narrow room where I had never been before. It was quite dark and on both sides were two wooden racks, one just above the floor and the other at eye level. I saw the outline of the bodies under the sheets and started to count them: one, two, three, four, five, six, seven. I counted again and again there were only seven. But then I turned around and walked straight into a cold foot sticking out from under a white cover. I had found the eighth body, and I ran out of the morgue into the daylight and across to my room, where I fell on the bed and hid my face in the pillow.

The next day at work I felt ill and had to lie down. Another woman took over my job for the day. I felt the dreaded oedema coming on. I had seen so many people die of it quickly, their bodies bloated and water-logged. My feet started to swell first, then my ankles and my sticklike lower legs, and next my thighs. I could actually see the process taking place, slowly, seemingly unstoppable.

Please, God, help me, I prayed, and I looked up at the ceiling and through the open door into the garden. The sun was shining as I felt my life ebbing away. When the children came in after school, my lower abdomen was swollen and hard to the touch.

Eva returned from her cleaning job some time later and she and the children took their bowls to collect the meal. That day it was an extra-large helping of thick mung-bean soup, a delicacy we had not laid eyes on for some years. It was a concentrated vitamin-B meal and for me it came just in the nick of time. I started passing water like a tap had been turned on, scarcely making it to the toilet block each time; as soon as I lay down in my room again, I had to get up once more and repeat the performance. I was up and down all night. There was a full moon outside and sharp shadows fell across the open corridor leading to the toilet block. I was very light-headed but jubilant, knowing that the liquid was leaving my body as quickly and dramatically as it had accumulated.

When morning came and the first light streamed in, my exhausted body was as thin as it had been twenty-four hours before. I was saved for the time being and Eva and the children held me and kissed me. That day I remained very weak but the next morning I felt my energy returning. I went back to the garden and filled my basket with green branches and flowers.

I had seen once more—this time at first hand—how precarious was the balance between life and death. One meal taken away from a starving person could mean the end, while an extra-nourishing bowl of food just at the right time could revive a dying person. It was a sobering thought. I knew I must not fail my children. I had taken to praying constantly an inward, silent prayer: Please help me, please help me, please help me.

A few months later, in August 1945, suddenly, stealthily, a whispered rumour started to do the rounds. An incredible, unbelievable rumour, but persistent. Somewhere in Japan, it went, a bomb had been dropped by the Americans, a bomb so devastating that its hideous effect had called an immediate halt to the war; the Japanese had surrendered, the war in the Pacific was over, soon we would be free. It was as if an electric wave of agitation, a suppressed feeling of jubilation, went trembling through the camp.

Having nurtured our dream of freedom for so many years, we hardly dared to believe it might be true. What if it were a plot? What if the Japanese were to observe our reactions and squash our hopes and expectations with cruel measures? After all we had heard it whispered that the military command planned to liquidate all prisoners, if events in the Pacific changed and they began losing the war.

We were careful not to show much agitation—it was essential that we kept our emotions under control. It was very hard to do, adrenalin was surging through our systems. For so long we had been starved of news from the outside world, and now the incredible was bursting in upon us. We pretended that nothing special had happened, but whispered amongst ourselves and impressed upon the children to be very careful and not to talk about anything they may have overheard.

Strange things started to happen. A few days after the rumours began, the more notorious and cruel of the Japanese overlords suddenly disappeared. Fukue was nowhere to be seen and some other military also disappeared without trace. Mizukuchi and a handful of the more moderate administrators took over from the military command and there was a long meeting behind closed doors between Mizukuchi and the Dutch doctor. When our doctor emerged he called together all the workers and the few patients who could walk. It was the evening of 15 August. In a voice trembling with emotion he told us that the Japanese had surrendered to the Allied forces, the fighting had ceased and we were free.

The scenes that followed still move me

deeply. It was exactly as I had often imagined the end would happen—suddenly. Now that long-awaited moment was here, it felt like an hallucination, a dream I would wake up from with a jolt to confront the old despair.

Women cried, their faces wet with tears. We embraced one another, and in the light of the lamps in the corridor we looked at each other, crying and laughing all at once. I held my children close to me and Eva and I tried to explain to them what had happened. But words failed us and I ended up repeating over and over again: 'We are free! We are free!'

The nurses hurried back to their patients and the workers followed them and quickly spread the word: 'The war is over. We are free!' Some patients were so excited that they wanted to get up and join in the celebration, but for most of them it was all too much. Some sobbed quietly, knowing that liberation for them had come too late.

We were too excited to go to sleep and in the corridors and on the garden paths in the moonlight women and children stood around in groups, discussing events and wondering what would happen next. Time was needed for the wonderful reality to sink in. Freedom, what did it mean? Could we leave the camp now? Would we be able to contact our husbands, brothers, sons? And what about food? My God, food for our hungry children!

Food came—where from, we did not know.

The next day there were generous helpings of rice, fresh vegetables, bread (real bread!) and eggs and milk and big chunks of meat in the broth. We could not believe our eyes and we ate and ate and ate. We could go back for seconds, or more, if we wanted. Some people were violently ill afterwards and the doctor cautioned us to take it easy.

An American military plane marked with a red cross came flying low over the back garden and, after due warning, dropped a huge crate on the lawn. It cracked open and spilled an abundance of tinned and packaged food on to the grass. We had been held back during this exercise and watched with fascination from a respectful distance. Imagine surviving all those years of starvation and then being killed by some tins of liverwurst! The Dutch doctor, who was now in charge of the hospital camp, and some of his office staff organised the distribution of the food. There was cheese and pate, butter and powdered milk, canned peas and beans and corned beef, biscuits and large bars of chocolate. It was distributed as fairly as possible and everyone, worker and patient, was given a helping.

The rich food was undigestible for most of the patients, but how could anyone refuse them their rightful part of the bounty? Some suffered from their indulgence, but it helped others on the slow road to recovery.

A few months earlier the doctor had told

me that if ever we were liberated, I would have to be very careful about my intake of food. Because of the years of constant digestive troubles, he suggested I go to a sanatorium where I would slowly get used to sampling bigger and heavier meals. But how could I remember that advice when all this beautiful food was put in front of me: the big bowls of porridge with lots of milk and sugar, the many slices of bread, the boiled eggs, the cheese and tomatoes, the coffee—all to begin the day with? The midday and evening meals followed and what the children could not finish on their plates, I would not let go to waste. The result? My digestive system started to function normally again from the first day of the massive intake of food and my gastric troubles ended overnight. Our good doctor shook his head and spread his hands and said: 'We hear of miracles all the time. Nothing seems to work according to the book. A lot of theories have been overturned. I am not surprised any more.'

It gave me great delight to see the children eat all the nice things they had been deprived of for so long; to see them lick their lips after a cup of warm cocoa in the morning; to watch them choose from the wide variety of fruit set out in large bowls on the long table in the shade of the banyan tree.

Medication was flown in, and there were clean bandages and huge quantities of disinfectant, bars of soap, and washing powder. How curious it was to see all these everyday items, taken for granted in normal times, greeted now with such enthusiasm and surprise, as if we had forgotten what they looked like.

The war was over and freedom was ours, but how were we going to use it? Where to start? How was society going to reorganise itself? We were not prisoners any more and we were going to rebuild the world. As free citizens we could now open the big gates of our prison. And that was precisely what we did.

CHAPTER TWELVE

The big gates of the prison camp were pushed open the day after the announcement that the war had ended. I remember holding hands with the children and Eva. Together we approached the exit slowly in the throng of excited women. Some of the nursing staff who could leave their patients for a few moments came too to sample the feeling of freedom which flowed in from the busy road outside. Some patients also wanted to walk through the gates even if it meant it would be the last steps they would ever take.

Outside, the footpath was packed with

Indonesians, most of them women and children, and we had to push our way through. They called out, laughing and crying, they grabbed our hands and tugged at our clothes, they offered us chickens and fruit and flowers. Their spontaneous show of affection was overwhelming and there were not many dry eyes.

The traffic slowed down and eventually stopped as we were escorted in triumph across the street to the *kampong*, the native village, where people came out of their houses to greet us or offer us tea and cold drinks. The children especially were lavished with kindness and Peter and Nelleke, being the smaller ones, were whisked away and shown around. I walked as in a dream, this was like olden times—it is difficult to find the words for how it felt.

We walked between the houses, we listened to the familiar sounds of the pounding of rice in the huge wooden vessels, the homely coo-cooing of the turtledoves in bamboo cages, and stopped now and then to talk to people and admire the beautiful big-eyed babies. I remember a large pond with ducks on it and shady trees all around. The children were delighted to see a few scraggy dogs, some very thin cats and a white cockatoo on a swing. After a while we decided to go back. We were not in a hurry, but I knew that I had to make my wreaths for the day as life—and death—

went on in the camp.

Communication with the other camps was established and notes were exchanged via the food trucks. To my great relief I heard that Mart and Maryke had survived the horrors of Tjideng and so had Georgette and her little daughter. A few days later word came from the other prisons outside Jakarta, and it turned out that my sister-in-law Karsia and her children had made it against all expectations.

Physical contact with the other camps was still impossible, however, because the immediate political and military situation was not at all clear. The Dutch authorities who had surrendered in March 1942 had been shipped away from Indonesia and so were not available to take the helm once more. The leadership vacuum was filled by the English, who arrived soon after 15 August. They tried to establish law and order in a country that had gone through a lot of turmoil in three years. Fighting erupted in the streets of Jakarta, and the English troops tried to quell small sporadic uprisings.

During the Japanese reign the Indonesian Nationalist Party, seeking independence from the Dutch, had the opportunity to organise itself properly, even though it was kept harshly under control by the rulers. After the Japanese surrendered, a great quantity of arms came into the hands of the Nationalists. With my own eyes I saw how many weapons were uncovered under a load of ice-blocks arriving in a truck at St Vincentius, where the Japanese were now prisoners of war. If the weapons had not been discovered when they were, the truck would have been driven to an outlying *kampong* and the arms delivered to the Nationalists. And as I later heard a Dutch official say: 'One youth with a rifle in his hand can command and terrorise a whole *kampong*.'

Most Japanese now kept a low profile. Although generally they had been terrible masters, they were perfect prisoners, fulfilling their duties as guards of the camp eagerly, glad that they were still able to move around. There came an end to their relative freedom when Ghurka soldiers were brought in from the former war zone in Burma. These took over the guard duties and the Japanese were taken away and imprisoned. Before this happened, however, the situation in Jakarta and, as we heard later, also in the other big cities on Java deteriorated to the point that the gate of our camp had to be closed to protect us from sporadic attacks by the Nationalist Indonesians. The Japanese guards were just as scared as we were when hand-grenades were thrown across the fence into the back garden and rifle shots rang out during the night.

One evening was particularly harrowing, I recall, and I shoved the children under the beds to keep them low. I was terribly scared, but eventually English troops came to our assistance and drove off the attackers. That must have been about two months after the gates had opened for the first time; it was terribly sad that we had to barricade ourselves against attacks by Indonesians we thought were our friends.

But as happens everywhere in the world, the protagonists in the struggle for independence fought on relentlessly and ruthlessly. A few gruesomely mutilated bodies were brought into the hospital, and some Eurasian families and Indonesians who had felt loyal to the Dutch sought protection in the camp from the horrifying persecution. Although we were now 'free'—and we had plenty to eat, and clothes and shoes, and expert medical care—we often lived in fear of our lives.

Some reunions with husbands or sons had taken place in the camp. Civilian men had been imprisoned in camps in West Java and it turned out there had been quite a few of these not far from St Vincentius. Husbands traced their wives to our hospital, thanks to the untiring efforts of the Red Cross . . . so much joy to see people separated for so long fall in each other's arms and hold each other as if they never wanted to let go again. Karsia sent me a note to tell me that my brother Bill had survived the gruelling years and that he had already joined her and the family.

The Red Cross lists contained the names of the surviving and perished POWs. They came from all the different camps in Indonesia, Burma, Thailand, Korea and Japan. John's name was on the survivor's list from Burma. Burma!—the truth of his having been shipped to such a faraway country hit me hard. Naturally my main emotion was of profound relief, although I realised there and then that I had never for a moment doubted that he was alive. I remembered that I often had been adamant in maintaining that, if his name had failed to be on the list of the living at the end of the war, this failure would prove to be a mistake by the authorities: John would make it, no question about that.

Amidst the rejoicing, there was the silent grief of the women who had not found their men's names on the lists of survivors. My brother Jan had died, leaving a very distraught wife and two young daughters, but I heard that much later on as there was no contact with Bandung for some time.

Letters began arriving at St Vincentius from husbands and other male relatives. John had been liberated from a prison camp in Thailand after tortuous years on the infamous Burma railroad and, being a Signal officer, became attached to the English Headquarters in Bangkok. His letters to me were full of love, but they became increasingly anxious about our safety. I had written to him at the first opportunity and had kept on writing and answering his letters but he had received none of them. He knew from the Red Cross lists that we were alive at the time of the Japanese surrender, but while his friends received letters from their loved ones in different camps on Java, no sign of life from me came his way. When I realised this predicament I felt helpless and near to tears.

By chance one day his torture ended, and I quote John's words so far as I can remember them. 'I was really at the end of my tether. My friends showed me the letters their wives had sent them and I turned away and locked myself in my room. By day I did my work and at night I refused to go out with my colleagues and have a good time. The thoughts tumbled through my head, turning and turning around the same question: What has happened to them? Are they alive? Why doesn't Nell write? until I thought I was slowly going mad. Then one day I had to go to the barracks at the other end of the city and this fellow at the desk looks up at me and says: "You are van de Graaff, aren't you? We have a little stack of letters for you. They have been delivered at the wrong office. We were going to send them over to Headquarters. Sorry about that."'

John stood there with the bundle of my letters in his hands; he went hot and he went cold, he jumped into his jeep and raced across the city. At his barracks in the privacy of his room he read and re-read my letters, One can only guess at the magnitude of the feelings that welled up in him.

From Mart I heard that her husband, who had been manager of a well-known hotel in Middle Java before the war, had been released from a civilian men's camp and immediately put in charge of the biggest hotel in Jakarta. She and Maryke were going to join him, and she asked if I could in any way manage to contact her there. That happened rather shortly after the end of the war was announced, before the situation in the streets developed into civil unrest. Enquiring if there was any possibility of transport into Jakarta, I was told that the safest way was to go in one of the food trucks and, once in the city, by military jeep to the hotel. I so much wanted to see Mart and meet her husband and I was excited at the thought of going all the way through the city I had known so well as a girl.

It was a hard decision to make, but I knew the children would be safe with Eva and my friends and the lure of adventure was strong. So I went in the food truck to Jakarta, where an English man took me in a military jeep to the hotel, where he had to attend a conference. It was exciting and frightening at the same time. Everywhere there were military vehicles, the city parks were in a shambles, the streets badly in need of repair and Indonesians, poorly dressed and looking hungry, were thronging along the footpaths or sitting in groups in the shade of the huge banyan trees.

To see Mart again and hold her and Maryke against me was worth the risk, and meeting her husband a delight. He held me at arm's length and said: 'I can't believe it, you are Mart's twin sister!'

The big Hotel des Indes was one of the first buildings to function normally again (it was kept in style by the Japanese during the occupation) and I was overawed by what was for us ex-prisoners a luxurious establishment. And a real meal in a dining room, with waiters, was an experience not quickly forgotten.

When I left the hotel I decided to visit one of the shops I had seen in passing on my way there, as I wanted to buy material to make some clothes for the children. They had to look splendid when they met their father! I had money to pay for it as everyone in the camp had received a small weekly allowance since the surrender. Where it came from I no longer remember but it was certainly a thrill to have some cash in my purse and the freedom to spend it. The shops, by pre-war standards, were very poorly stocked but to me they sold a rich variety of goods. I chose some beautiful pink gingham for the girls' dresses and bought blue shorts for the two boys.

On my way back to the place where I had arranged to meet a military escort that would take me 'home' to St Vincentius, I almost ran into a truck coming towards me at great speed.

Only by pressing myself against the wall lining the street did I escape certain death by a few inches. I glimpsed the grinning faces of two young Indonesians in the cabin, murderous intent glinting in their eyes. Back in the camp I heard of instances in which some European women, tempted to go shopping in the city had been dragged into a side lane or pulled through a hidden door and had not been heard of since. These reports of kidnapping and my own experience killed any further desire to go exploring and I stayed in the relative safety of St Vincentius.

When the Japanese officers and the administrators were taken prisoner by the English, the only Japanese walking around free was Dr Mizukuchi, the man who had done his utmost to soften harsh directions from the Japanese military command and who had tried in his own unobtrusive way to make life under the oppressor a bit more bearable for us. A petition urging that he be allowed to go free and stating the reasons had been sent to the English commander, signed by all the workers, nursing staff and patients able to write, and of course by our own Dutch doctor who was now in charge of the hospital camp. Mizukuchi kept very much to himself. Although we saw him occasionally he stayed most of the time in his own quarters.

About a week after our liberation, we all assembled on the lawn in the back garden to watch the official raising of the Dutch flag. A lonely figure in Japanese uniform, walked slowly towards our group of deeply moved people about to witness the crowning of their newfound freedom. A hush of silence came over us when we saw him and in a spontaneous gesture we bowed towards him. With a deep bow he acknowledged our courtesy. Later we heard that he had made a special request to be allowed to attend the ceremony. And when the tricolour was raised and we sang the Dutch national anthem, he stood ramrod still, saluting the flag. We had all heard that his hometown was Hiroshima.

CHAPTER THIRTEEN

Those of us in the camp who had not yet been reunited with our husbands started getting impatient as we wondered what in heaven's name was keeping them from us for so long. Political considerations prevented the Dutch administration and the Dutch military, exiled by the Japanese, from returning yet to Indonesia and during this time the situation, on Java especially, deteriorated by the day. It was several months before the frustrated Dutch were able to leave their enforced exile and join their anxious families and return to work. However, a golden opportunity presented itself for many women to make use of the empty transport ships that returned to Thailand to bring more Ghurkas down to Indonesia.

Some enterprising people in the camps had organised a request to the English commander in Jakarta to accept Dutch women and children on board the ships bound for Bangkok, where most of the ex-prisoners of war from that region of the world were waiting. When we found out in early December that our names were on the list of women whose husbands were still in Bangkok and who had requested transport there at the first available opportunity, we were in a state of almost unbearable anxiety and excitement. The thought that maybe within a few weeks I would be able to see John, to hold him, to show him his children, sent shivers along my spine. I just could not believe that that event, ending those long years of separation, would eventually take place.

I busied myself finishing off the girls' dresses and shirts for the boys to match their blue shorts. In a small suitcase I obtained, I packed all the new clothes, the drawings that the children had made for their father, and some new handkerchiefs wrapped in cellophane, a little present for him.

I had already discarded the flimsy dress I had carted around for so long, having bought something more appropriate from a woman who, wisely, had set up a small dress shop in the camp; and we all had a pair of shoes, purchased from another enterprising businesswoman. We were now able to buy articles of all kinds from the small shops that had sprung up in the camp.

It was mid-December and we were totally prepared to pick up our few belongings and leave the camp at a moment's notice when the word came that our ship was set to sail. We were warned by the camp authorities that the journey in open trucks from St Vincentius to Tandjong Priok, the harbour of Jakarta, would be risky; we could encounter all sorts of difficulties, the worst being if we were waylaid and attacked by guerillas. A strong escort of armed men would accompany us, we were told, and we could only trust our luck.

I had informed Bill and Karsia and also Mart that we might have to leave at short notice. I knew also that the English commander in Jakarta would notify Bangkok if and when a shipload of women and children could be expected to arrive. On about 17 December the excitement rose to a fever pitch when suddenly we heard that we had to be ready the next morning at the crack of dawn. At last the great moment had arrived.

That night Johnny went down with a high temperature—he was delirious. The doctor examined him and shook his head. 'I don't know what causes this fever,' he said as he looked at me with pity and compassion. 'I would advise you not to leave tomorrow, the risk of taking such a sick child on board an overcrowded ship is really too great.'

I sat on the floor next to Johnny's bed, his hot little hand in mine, and felt an icy chill creep around my heart. I looked up at the kind doctor, pleading with him: 'But we have to go, doctor, my husband will be waiting. I don't know if we would get another chance.' He packed his little bag, patted me on the head and, as he was leaving, turned and said: 'If you take him, it will be at your own risk. I advise you not to go—' I sat for hours with Johnny, changing the cool, wet cloths on his forehead, holding his hand and praying as only a desperate mother and wife could pray.

Towards morning the fever had left his body and he sat up shakily and smiled. We all dressed in record time, gulped down some drinks and packed fruit and a few sandwiches. I had to sit on the poor little suitcase to make it close, and we hurried to the big entrance gate where two open trucks were waiting. The good doctor looked doubtful but he admitted that Johnny had indeed recovered and wished us a safe journey. So did the other people staying behind who came to wave and wish us luck. The two trucks were packed. We were standing up and had to hold on to each other as the vehicles gathered speed.

One of the most dangerous points we had to negotiate was the train overpass, only about five minutes from the hospital. This viaduct was a disputed strategic point between the English troops and the guerillas and it had changed hands a few times. The latest information was that the Nationalists had acquired a foothold high above the road and we had been instructed to crouch down as low as possible when we approached the overpass. The trucks would go at full speed under the dangerous bridge and through to the other side. Obeying the orders, we all ducked down. I pushed the children on to the floor and tried to cover them as much as possible with my body. Our guards aimed their tommy-guns at the treacherous overpass and the trucks rumbled speedily, and safely, to the other side. We sighed with relief and managed to reach the docks without further disturbance.

On the wharf groups of women and children were already assembled from other places in Jakarta, St Vincentius being the remotest camp. The English cargo ship on which we were to sail was being unloaded, the main cargo being Ghurkas who had come straight from Burma where they had had their share of fighting the enemy. My children liked the Ghurkas as many of them had already taken over guarding our camp. The children loved sitting around the fire when the smiling warriors shared their delicious chapattis with them. After all the Ghurkas had disembarked, the hundreds and hundreds of women and children walked up the gangplanks. We were accommodated in the holds of the small ship, where rats and cockroaches scurried away at our approach and the smell of unwashed bodies and overburdened toilets welcomed us. The dark holds had been a home for the soldiers for several days or possibly weeks.

Hammocks, strung up above long tables, were folded up when food was distributed at mealtimes. I secured one table with four hammocks fastened above it. At night I slept on the table while the children, much to their delight, swayed above me. In a stern voice I had to call them to order, and for a while they were perfectly still; one of them soon started to move slowly, then faster, so that his or her hammock touched another, which in turn started to sway, until all four were moving in perfect rhythm to and fro.

Notwithstanding the cramped and terribly unhygienic conditions, we were all very excited to be at last on the ship that would reunite us with our loved ones. The journey lasted about five or six days. Sometimes in rough weather we had to crawl on to the deck because the smell of people being seasick in the holds was more than we could bear. Most days it was sunny and calm and every inch of the deck was taken up by the body of a woman or child. The Indian crew were constantly busy chasing children away from places they should not have been in or plucking them from the rigging. Not one child fell overboard, thanks to the watchfulness of the Indians and the constant supervision of anxious mothers.

I remember sitting on the deck one morning, hemmed in on all sides, sewing the last buttons on the girls' dresses. Every so often I looked up, counting my children who were having the time of their lives with so many playmates. The wind was ruffling their hair, the sun was shining and the blue expanse of the heavens formed a perfect canopy above the small ship steadily ploughing on towards our destination. Each time I counted: one, two, three, four. I kept watch like a hawk, not wanting to let any of them stray out of sight. Looking up once, I located Johnny, and there was Nelleke holding on to Manya's hand and . . . where was Peter? I could not spot my sturdy, adventurous four-year-old amongst the children, but then I looked up. On the flat, broad top part of the railing my son was balancing on his stomach, his bottom and legs dangling above the deck, his head and arms limp, high above the heaving sea. Completely at ease, he was looking down with great interest at the turbulent water. One little bump from the excited children would have made him lose his balance and topple over the side. In a split second I dropped my sewing and in one great leap was at the railing where I snatched him back to safety. I gave him one good smack on his bottom and burst into tears. He did not cry, but looked flabbergasted as I had almost never spanked my children. He only wanted to have a good look at the waves, he said. For months afterwards, if I thought of that critical moment, my stomach tightened and my heart missed a beat.

I had watched Johnny closely for the first few days after his fever but, although he was a bit shaky and pale for the first twenty-four hours, he continued to remain well. Nelleke showed signs of the mild form of oedema, her little face round and her tummy a bit extended, but during the next months she lost those signs of the prison camp. I had gained abnormally in weight since the food situation had changed. In the first six weeks I gained 20 kilograms and looked anything but emaciated. Much of that weight was fluid—it was a phenomenon that similarly affected many women in the same circumstances. At least my wish to appear rounded and healthy-looking for John would be fulfilled.

We were wearing our old clothes on the ship—it would have been pointless to do otherwise. The new ones were neatly folded away, waiting for the moment of arrival. We neared Bangkok late at night on 23 December 1945. The sea was calm and a full moon was sending silver beams down on to the water where they became myriads of crystals, dancing and glistening. Emotions can become so overpowering that they throw you into a turmoil of feelings that may be almost unbearable. At that point you become suddenly very calm—it is the only way to cope with the situation—and deep down you know that you will receive the strength to sustain you, be it in deepest sorrow or in ecstatic joy.

Early on 24 December—Christmas Eve and Johnny's 8th birthday—the pilot manoeuvred us into the harbour and we berthed at the dock. I stood with my children at the railing, all beautifully dressed, all holding on to each other. Although it was already very hot and humid, my hands were like ice, and I scanned the crowd on the wharf for the tall, commanding figure in uniform who would be waiting for us. I saw many men in uniform, but could not distinguish John among them. The children pulled my hands and my dress, craned their necks and called out above the noise of machinery and voices: Mummy, where is Dad? Do you see him? Where is Daddy, Mum?

When the customs personnel arrived on board, I saw with them a Dutch officer who came straight across to me. I recognised him as a colleague of John's. He greeted us affectionately and told us that John had had to attend an urgent staff meeting and had asked him to take me to the hotel where we were booked in. Of course there was a momentary feeling of being let down—we had been so keyed up—but on the other hand it gave us a bit of breathing space in which to prepare for the great moment.

Leo took us in his jeep through the streets of Bangkok and what a joyful feeling it was to be in a city where freedom was the normal state of affairs. No fear of snipers, of sudden attacks, people waved to us, the sun was shining, we were free and we were going to see the husband and father we had dreamt about for so long. At the Hotel Trocadero, a very large and impressive hotel which had been transformed into a receiving depot for the evacuees, I was shown to a spacious room on the third floor. There were several single mattresses on the floor and a double mattress in the corner, all of them neatly shrouded in mosquito nets. I thanked Leo for his care and he hurried back to the barracks, from where he would let John know we had arrived safely.

It was exciting to be in a real hotel, to have such a comfortable room at our disposal and a big bathroom at the end of the corridor. What luxury!

We stood on the balcony and looked down on the street, with its teeming crowds, loudly honking cars and foodstalls with an abundance of colourful fruit. Having unpacked our suitcase, we refreshed ourselves in the bathroom and admired ourselves in the long mirror. I adjusted the ribbons in the girls' hair, brushed the boys' unruly mops and put some extra powder on my nose. Back in our room we were restless—we kept sitting down and getting up again—but we did not dare leave the room because it was our meeting place.

I tried to breathe deeply and calm my racing heart, and Johnny slipped out of the room. John told me later how he was led straight to our room when he came out of the lift on the third floor. In the long, dimly lit hallway he saw a thin boy coming towards him who said: 'Hello, Daddy, I am Johnny and I'll take you to Mummy's room.' The door opened and they walked in, hand in hand.

Again, words fail me in trying to describe this encounter after a three and a half year separation. Our eyes were hungry for each other, trying to take in the beloved features missed so greatly during that long time. And the thrill of being able to show John his children who had grown beyond recognition during those years, who had survived and were now healthy and well! They clung to him as if to make sure he was real at last. And then his fourth child whom he had never set eyes upon yet. I lifted her in my arms so that he could feast his gaze upon her. He approached her very gently and she was coy, hiding her face against my shoulder and glancing at him from underneath her long eyelashes. Then she suddenly straightened herself and put out her arms towards him.

All these moments are held fast in my memory as so many precious stones set in a glittering diadem.

John had a bag with him out of which he produced a bottle of perfume for me and a present for each of the children that he had prepared with so much love in the weeks before our arrival. He had bought two beautiful large dolls for the girls, made out of soft material by a Swiss woman who lived in Bangkok; they came complete with a change of lovely clothes. Johnny received a handcrafted wooden train, the engine and carriages painted in glossy colours. For Peter there was a box of building blocks in all shapes and colours, made by the same woodcarver. Time and time again the children went to their father to embrace him and he looked across their heads towards me with an expression I will never forget.

How did Johnny recognise his father immediately? 'I saw it was you from the photo,' he said. This photo I still have in my possession, it is very frail and here and there kept together with cellotape. It was taken in Surabaya by an American war correspondent who stayed with us for a few days before the war reached Java. It pictured John from the waist up in his uniform and it was a marvellous likeness, with a hint of the humorous smile in his eyes and around his mouth that was so typical. This photo was kissed goodnight for three and a half years by four eager children and it survived all the tribulations of war to help Johnny identify his father.

We all went down to dinner in the huge dining room and afterwards we put to bed four very tired, happy children. John and I only fell into a deep sleep towards morning. Between embraces we talked and talked, slept fitfully for a while, made love again, and talked and talked. We held each other and looked each other in the eyes, and we realised that in neither of us was there a feeling of hatred for our Japanese oppressors, only an all-encompassing feeling of sadness and compassion for all victims of the war, be they the conquerors or the vanquished.

CHAPTER FOURTEEN

To write about the events that followed in Bangkok would fill another book. The bizarre things that happened to us during our four month stay there could have come straight out of an adventure thriller.

When we made it back to Indonesia, John was attached to Headquarters in Surabaya, and we lived in a comfortable house next door to the imposing Headquarters building.

Surabaya was partly in shambles after the war and life seemed to be a never ending story of danger and uncertainty. Drinking water supplies, for example, had to be shipped in from Singapore as the Indonesian guerillas who surrounded the city had taken possession of the city's reservoirs in the countryside beyond. We learned to live with constant and often unexpected danger.

Our fifth child Albert was born in December 1946, and while I was in the delivery room at the hospital, which was near the outskirts of the city, I heard the loud boom-boom of heavy artillery. Many wounded were carried along the passage past the maternity ward that day.

In April 1947 the children and I boarded an evacuation ship bound for the Netherlands. After a stopover in Jakarta to pick up other women and children and some very sick men, we set sail. The last time I had set foot on Dutch soil had been in 1936 when, as newlyweds, John and I were heading off for a new life together in Indonesia. So much had happened in the eleven years in between, in Europe and in the East, that it seemed a lifetime had passed since we had seen those we left behind. The reunions with my parents and relatives were very emotional.

Mart and her little family had returned for good. Bill and Karsia and their children had been repatriated earlier than I, so also my brother Jan's wife and her two daughters; they had all more or less settled down in the old country. Georgette and her husband and daughter lived not far from my parents. Of course meeting up with them all again, after sharing so many agonising years, brought back many memories. We rejoiced with the survivors and mourned for those who had not made it.

John had stayed back in Surabaya, where he was still needed at Headquarters. He joined us just before Christmas and four months later we flew back to Indonesia, where we lived in Bandung for a couple of years. I again returned to Holland with the children when John was transferred to Hollandia, the capital of Dutch New Guinea, as it was then known. He joined us a few months later in 1950 and we had to make the agonising decision about what to do with our future, Indonesia having become independent by then.

John could have joined the Netherlands Army, the Dutch Civil Service, or a private company—experienced staff were urgently needed everywhere. His father offered him the directorship of the family business, an engineering bureau, but he declined. We both realised that after our many eventful years it would be hard to settle into a quiet, ordered life. Although beautiful and historically rich, Holland was a small densely populated country, where life seemed to us too restricted, too regulated. We thought back with nostalgia to the openness of the countryside of Java, the majestic mountains, the lush ricefields, the warm, sunny climate. But we could not go back there because there was no suitable work for John and because of the backlash against the Dutch in the wake of independence.

Even the uncertainty and the unavoidable element of danger during our last few years on Java after the war seemed to us preferable to a staid life in an ordered society. At the mere whiff of adventure or unknown possibilities we would look at each other with the unspoken question: Will we pack up again and go?

Apparently quite a few of the thousands of people who were repatriated from Indonesia faced the same dilemma. Many left Holland to try to find a new life overseas, in Australia, New Zealand, Brazil or Canada. As we heard very favourable reports about the possibilities for work in Australia, and maybe also because of its proximity to Indonesia, we decided to emigrate there.

Saying goodbye to our families and friends caused many heartaches. Quite a few expressed their disapproval of the gigantic step into uncertainty we were taking with our large young family (I was expecting our sixth child then) when good positions and security were being offered in the mother country. But we had made up our minds and towards the end of April 1951, we boarded the plane for Australia.

After arriving in Sydney we made the spectacular train journey through the Blue Mountains west to Bathurst. There we entered the migration camp outside the city which was to be home for about seven months.

Waking up early on the first morning, I walked outside. I felt the sunshine on my face and looked across at the mountains in the distance and the hilly countryside around me; I listened to the unfamiliar birdsongs and breathed in the smell of a strange country. The light too had an unfamiliar quality. I knew that I would love living here.

I walked on to see the surrounding countryside better—the far mountains, the hazy horizon—and I was overawed by the vastness of the land and by how ancient it seemed. I stood still in mystical communion with the soil, the plants, the trees and the animals, until John and the children found me and took me back to the large communal dining hall for breakfast.

After a few days John went to Melbourne to start building the prefabricated house we had bought in Holland and which was being shipped over. He only came back to Bathurst for a short time when our son Bill was born at the beginning of June, overjoyed that our sixth child had come into the world without complications. We left Bathurst camp towards the end of 1951 and joined John, who had rented a ramshackle old place in Croydon, near Melbourne, and was busy finishing off the house.

Our life together as a family began once more, with all the ups and downs one would expect from arriving in a new country and having to adjust to new customs and a different lifestyle. The first five years were very difficult financially. John tried his hand at all sorts of jobs and when Bill was eighteen months old I helped keep the homefires burning by working as a nursing aid in a hospital. All the children pulled their weight in the household, by babysitting for their little brother or earning some extra money doing odd jobs. It really was a family effort.

At the end of the five years John was able to start on a teaching career on the strength of his qualifications as a military engineer. For the next fifteen years he taught secondary school Mathematics and Physics, first in Victoria and later in Sydney.

Our financial situation improved considerably, not least because the four older children had become independent, deciding to obtain jobs and further their schooling part-time. As they married, there were grandchildren—Australia was home for us now, and life was full with its dramas and comedies, its occasional frustrations and wholly pleasing events.

John and I reminisced about the past now and then, about the terror of the years in prison and the cruel separation from each other. We lived in full awareness of the good things that happened to us every new day, we were conscious of the miracle that had brought us together again, and of our good fortune in seeing the children grow up so healthy and strong. We did not take anything for granted, but tried to live every day to the full.

The blow came unexpectedly and with awful finality. Just at midnight on 28 January 1970, John suffered a massive heart attack which ended his life there and then. For the last few weeks his heart had made him slightly uncomfortable and the doctor had told him to take it a bit easy. But this attack on the life of this strong and active man was completely unexpected, and I had to summon all my strength to be able to accept the loss of him and to adjust to living without my constant companion.

Of the two younger children Albert had married but Bill was still living with me and attending university when John died. With the modest proceeds of a life insurance policy, I bought a small unit overlooking Sydney Harbour and we left the big rented place we had lived in for many years where I encountered memories of John at every step of the stairs, in every corner of the rooms. I had been working full-time for several years with a large marketing research firm—it was a very demanding, busy job, but now it helped me to cope with my changed lifestyle. I buried myself in my work at the office and often worked there until late at night.

The love and affection of my children was what really kept me going during that first difficult year. I was so lucky that Bill was staying with me, while Albert and his wife had a flat in the same street and Manya lived with her husband and young son only ten minutes away. Johnny and his wife lived in Melbourne, as did Peter, his wife and their two small children, while Nelleke's home, with husband and two sons, was in Queensland.

Gradually, towards the end of the first year, with summer approaching and the sunny days getting longer, the traumatic experience of my sudden grief was losing its sharp edges; I felt that life was again demanding my attention.

I started to go to the swimming pool down the road, picked up my tennis racquet again, and looked around me with renewed interest. I made many new friends while maintaining the bonds with the old, trusted ones. I had so much to live for, not in the least my beautiful family, and I knew I was blessed with a great curiosity for new things, an insatiable thirst for unexplored territory, both physical and mental. Being alone, I had plenty of opportunity to contemplate the past. I remembered the time in the little cottage among the ricefields in Nagrok, and remembered the devotion and help of Atik, Tjètjè and Apit in those critical times. And the more I thought about it the smaller the distance seemed to become between Australia and Java. It was as if I could touch the whitewashed walls of the humble cottage and in my imagination I saw myself overlooking the intense green of the terraced ricefields. I heard the women pounding rice in wooden vessels, I heard turtle doves in bamboo cages, I saw the faces of the three men, my friends, light up when they came down the path to greet me. An unbearable longing overcame me—I wanted to be back there to thank them for what they had done for me and the children. I wanted to say to them: 'Look here at what you have achieved. Without your help I would not be today a fulfilled woman, richly blessed by her children and so rich in experience. Without you I might not have lived to tell the tale of the sweetness and the harshness of the years that followed our parting so long, long ago.' I dearly wanted to make my fantasy come true, to pack my suitcase and fly to Indonesia.

Don't wait any longer, I counselled myself. You have waited long enough. You will never have peace of mind if you don't try to locate them now.

Why shouldn't I go now, I thought. I was independent, all my children were managing their own lives, there was nothing to hold me back. I knew that I could afford it, as I had worked very hard the whole year and had spent very little. The more I thought about it, the more excited I became. When I discussed my plan with the children, they were enthusiastic. And we knew that it would be safe. During the last ten years Indonesia's relationship with the Netherlands had improved to such an extent that several Dutch experts in the rubber, coffee and oil industries, to name only a few, had been invited back to Indonesia to provide assistance through their knowledge and experience. Indonesian-born Dutch, especially, were welcomed back with open arms and asked to help rebuild the country.

My heart started to speed up at the thought that I would go back to the land of my birth, to the people I felt so close to. I appreciated now the strong pull of childhood memories and how intimately they are bound up with that special place on earth, wherever it might be. I booked my ticket, packed my bags and counted the days to departure.

It was September 1971 when I left and my stay of four weeks would end just before the monsoon started and the rains come washing down in tropical deluge. I was ready for the experience of a lifetime.

CHAPTER FIFTEEN

The plane landed in Jakarta at sunset. It had been raining heavily, the tarmac was glistening, and dark clouds drifted by as the setting sun glowed on the western horizon. The warmth and humidity enveloped me as I emerged from the aircraft and the sounds and the smells of Indonesia made me feel I was coming home. In a flash I realised how much I had missed all this since I had left the country more than twenty years ago. I felt emotional, close to tears, and I could suddenly understand the grand gesture of expatriates who, returning to their homeland, kissed the ground on which their first faltering steps had fallen.

I had to adjust quickly to the jostling, noisy crowds and I was literally pushed into one of the waiting taxis by a driver keen to get a fare.

It was all so familiar to me, but I was taken aback by the size of the crowds, everywhere. The population of Jakarta had grown enormously since I was last there. I checked in to a large modern hotel recommended to me by a friend in Sydney. The accommodation was excellent, my room very large and everywhere fans on high ceilings wafted cool air.

From my third-floor balcony I looked down on a huge square surrounded by tall, modern buildings. The street noises, the hum of the big city where life seemed to go on at all hours of the day and night, drifted up to me, but this part of Jakarta had changed so much from my recollection of it. I felt a little wistful that the character of the sprawling, easygoing tropical city had been so drastically transformed by multi-storey buildings.

The feeling of being on familiar ground returned to me when I took a taxi to one of the older suburbs of Jakarta. The street lighting was bad, huge trees lined the road, it was very quiet and the driver had difficulty locating the address I sought. At last we arrived and I went up the stairs to the old-fashioned verandah where I called out to make my presence known. A homely, elderly lady in a smock and with grey hair drawn into a bun opened the door. Her sister, a good friend of mine in Melbourne, had given me her address and asked me to hand over a parcel. The old lady

160

welcomed me warmly and invited me to join her for supper which was just about to be served.

We sat in the dining room overlooking the garden. The wide-open windows brought in the evening breeze, heavy with the perfume of night-flowers, and the low-hung lamp threw a perfect circle of light on the white tablecloth. The crickets chirped their monotonous song and the frogs joined in, happy after the heavy rain.

The cook came out from the kitchen with fried eggs and a large glass jug of cold water filled with tinkling ice-cubes. I heard the soft patter of her bare feet on the marble floor, and her old dark face lit up in a delighted grin when I said *Selamat malam!* (good evening) to her.

I smelt the Chinese bread in the basket and the freshly brewed coffee, and I heard the distant calls of street vendors selling *sateh* and other delicacies from their mobile stalls. The sweetness of it all was almost too much to bear. How I loved this country—I felt I had come home.

The next morning, very early, I stood on the hotel balcony and saw the city awaken. There was not much traffic around yet and in the dawn light I noticed that there were still many houses squeezed in between the larger buildings. In a small canal with swiftly running water, a man was splashing his face with water and brushing his teeth; a little further upstream, two women, standing waist deep in the water, combed their long, black hair, their sarongs wrapped tightly around them; and, recalling the 'olden days', further upstream again a man squatted over the edge of the canal with his pants down. The cool water still served all their bodily needs, just as it had for their parents and grandparents.

Later that day I hired a taxi and asked the driver to take me outside the city to St Vincentius. The building was freshly painted and obviously well-looked after. The high ugly fences I remembered had gone and the garden was lush and green. The nuns had taken over again and clearly the convent school had been re-established. It all looked so prim and proper and peaceful, as if never an agonised sigh had been heard within its walls, as if the smell of death that had lingered around the sick wards was ever only in my imagination. The days of St Vincentius, hospital prison camp, seemed an age away now. In the twenty-five years since, much had occurred in my life and help in time of need had never been far away. I sighed and felt blessed, and asked the driver to take me next past the house I had lived in as a girl and the church where my father had been a minister. They were both still there, although in need of repair.

I had no desire to return to Tjideng.

My ultimate goal was to get to Nagrok,

where I hoped to be able to trace the whereabouts of Atik, Tjètjè and Apit. I realised there was only a slender hope of finding any of them alive. As a matter of fact, I had to admit to myself that trying to locate them amongst millions of Indonesians after an absence of thirty years, was probably worse than looking for a needle in a haystack. But I was determined to pursue my search. It was not so much a matter of being stubborn as feeling that I was being guided in this direction. It was something I just had to do, no question about it. I had an introductory letter and a parcel for friends of Peter's wife Glenys who lived in Bandung; they had been notified I would be coming.

Small private buses commuted daily between Jakarta and Bandung and early next morning I set off, squeezed in with about a dozen Indonesians. Next to me sat a young woman, obviously very tired, who apologised for leaning against me. It was towards the end of Ramadhan, the Muslim month of fasting from sunrise to sunset, and she told me that she could not keep her eyes open and promptly fell asleep against my shoulder.

The bus trip was terrifying, especially when we had to negotiate hairpin bends in the mountains in thick mist and on narrow, constantly winding roads. The driver went at top speed. I closed my eyes and said to myself: If it is my time, it is my time. I can't do anything about it.

Glenys's girlfriend was at home when I arrived. Her husband came in at lunchtime and together we discussed ways of getting to Nagrok. I also wanted to find out the best way to go to Djogja in Middle Java, which was near the former Dutch military base of Magelang, where John and I had lived before I fled in 1942. I would make it a sort of pilgrimage, as I was keen to visit the places that had played an important part in my life. After a couple of days with Glenys's friends, who became my friends also, I went to the part of Bandung that had become the Kareës prison camp. It was quiet and suburban now and the houses had all been restored as family homes. There was not even a hint of the turbulent times of yesteryear.

When I arrived in Djogja by train I took a taxi to the address given to me by the tourist bureau in Bandung. I had booked a room in a private home, which I was advised, would be a more convenient arrangement and in any case not as impersonal as hotel accommodation. It was a large old-fashioned home in the better part of Djogja, the residence of the widow of a well-known medical man. She had many wonderful photos of her and her husband in company with United States and European heads of state, a testimony to her husband's international standing. She was on the widow's pension but it was insufficient to maintain her

164

large home, so she rented some of the rooms and provided full board.

She was frail and elderly, and very kind and gracious. She served up delicious Indonesian dishes, and sat with me during my meals at the long carved table which was covered in immaculate white linen and set with heavy silver cutlery and crystal glassware. She would not eat with me, but had her meals later with her young relatives in the small dining room at the back of the house. I was the only guest at that time and during the two days I stayed with her, we opened our hearts to each other and found the time too short to exchange all our happy and sad experiences. The language we spoke was a curious mixture of English, Indonesian and Dutch. And it was delightful.

When already elderly, her husband used to ride a bicycle so that he could reach, undetected, wounded Indonesians fighting from ambushes. The Indonesian freedom-fighters were engaged in battle with the Dutch troops in Middle Java (in about 1948) and as John at that time was in charge of Signal Operations, we concluded that our husbands most probably were at the same time at the same place, but in opposing forces. She and I were both thankful that neither of them had been in positions that required them to shoot their opponents. The day after my arrival she was going for her weekly visit to the cemetery and asked me if I would like to accompany her. We travelled in her big old black car driven by her nephew. Stopping at the markets, we each bought an armful of flowers.

At the cemetery she spread a little mat on the fine gravel at the foot of her husband's grave. Her nephew had brought along an *anglo*, a small earthenware stove, in which he started a small fire on some coals and, sprinkling incense on the flames, placed the *anglo* at the head of the grave and we strewed our flowers liberally over the simple marble slab.

As we knelt on the mat, we bowed our heads and put our arms around each other's shoulders, praying for both our husbands and for all the dead and maimed and wounded in the war. Our tears mingled when our cheeks touched. And above all we prayed for peace. This was indeed a homecoming of a special kind.

The next day I went with her nephew to Magelang and there laid to rest many memories. I walked around and saw the old house and felt like a witness looking in upon a life far removed from my own.

When I arrived back in Bandung, I decided not to postpone my trip to Nagrok any longer. I would take the early morning train the next day to Sukabumi and from there go by *bemo*, a small three-wheeled vehicle, up the mountain road to Hotel Salabintana, where in 1942 I had met up with my brother Bill and his family.

From there I would start my inquiries. I knew that when I entered the hotel it would bring back sad memories but it seemed the logical place to begin to find out if anybody knew my three friends. After all, Nagrok was only on the other side of the ravine and Apit's house halfway down the road from Sukabumi.

I went to bed early that night, feeling charged with an energy I could not really explain. Perhaps I was receptive to this energy because I so much wished my mission to succeed. I meditated for about an hour, and prayed: Please let me find them. I could not sleep and felt as though I hovered all the time between full alertness and a curious dream state. At one point I had a vision—it was not a dream. It was like a framed picture—there was no movement—and every detail became imprinted on my mind. It was as if I looked down a narrow path which I knew led to a river. On both sides large smooth stones—or, rather, rocks—reflected an orange-purple light, and a thick stand of bamboo stood next to the road on the right. I just stared at it and then the picture faded and I must have fallen asleep. When I woke up in the early morning, the picture was still vivid but, wanting to make it to the train on time and use the day to the full, I dismissed it.

When I arrived in Sukabumi I selected a sturdy-looking *bemo*. When we had a full load of passengers, we set off on the long haul up the mountain road to Salabintana. I thought I remembered where Apit's small stone house backed on to the rice and corn fields, and I fervently hoped that he still lived there. But to my dismay and embarrassment I saw many identical houses lining the road all the way up to the hotel, and I reproached myself for being so naive as to think I would easily recognise Apit's house. In thirty years many new houses had been built along this busy road. I pinned my hopes for information on the staff of Salabintana and when I was dropped off in the driveway of the hotel, I had a look around before going to the reception desk. I had stood in the same place thirty long years ago and surveyed the same impressive scenery—the mighty mountain chain, the valley, the beautiful gardens. I was shown to the dining room where I ordered a fried rice with some side dishes. The waiter was a man from the island of Sulawesi, and, as I was born in the capital, Menado, we had an animated conversation. I told him the reason for my visit, but the names were unknown to him. 'But,' he said, 'there are some men from Nagrok working here in the garden. I'll go and see if they can tell me something.'

I waited out on the front lawn for him to return feeling hot and cold all over. I knew that what I was about to hear in a few moments was crucial: if people from Nagrok itself did not know what had happened to my friends, who then would be able to help me? The waiter returned slowly. When he stood in front of me he looked up, and with a sad face he said, almost apologetically: 'I am sorry, Madam, but they say that Atik and Tjètjè died and that Apit has gone and now lives in Jakarta, they don't know where.'

I stood stock-still and tried to take in what he had told me. My head said to me that this was the end of my search. But my heart spoke a different language, and would not so easily surrender to defeat. In my handbag were three envelopes containing money I wanted to give to my friends in appreciation of what they had done for me. Having come all this way, I just could not accept that it was all over now. I straightened myself, looked up into the blue sky and prayed silently for help.

Outwardly calm, I thanked the helpful waiter and asked him to call a *bemo* for me so that I could return to Sukabumi. He sent a messenger boy to hail one. Just as he reached the road one passed by. The driver had seen him calling out at the top of his voice and waving his arms, and he stopped and reversed up the driveway to where I was waiting. Getting in, I asked the driver: 'Would you, please, drive slowly on the way down? I want to see if I can recognise the house of Apit, the taxi-driver. I know that he has moved to Jakarta, but I still would like to have a look.' A passenger's voice replied from the back of the *bemo*: 'Apit has not moved to Jakarta. He still lives there. I am his son and I'll take you there.'

It felt as if an electrical stream flashed along my spine. I thought: This can't be true, I must be dreaming. The excited voices behind me told me I wasn't dreaming, and I told Apit's son that I had come especially all the way from Australia to find his father and to thank him for all that he had done for me thirty years ago. He looked around proudly to the other passengers and everybody talked at once, excited about the drama taking place in their midst.

Halfway down the road to Sukabumi the driver stopped in front of one of many identical houses. Apit's son jumped out and went quickly through the little front yard and up the steps on to the verandah. He came back with his mother. I got out and we looked each other in the eyes and held each other's hands. What moved me most was that she called me *'Njonja Manis'* (Sweet Lady), the endearing name they had given me when I lived in their village at the age of twenty-six. She took me in triumph to her house and all the passengers of the *bemo* and the driver crowded in the front yard while the neighbours on both sides leant over the hedges—nobody wanted to miss any of the excitement. Children were laughing and shouting, dogs barking, and the small front yard quickly became a muddy mess, as it had recently been raining.

Apit's wife explained to me that about fifteen years ago, at her persuasion, Apit had taken a second wife (like most Indonesians they were Muslims). She had given him her young niece to marry and she told me with great pride that they had now eight children. He lived just down the road with his wife, but the majority of the children were generally here.

She sent one of the youngsters to call *Bapa*, while her eldest daughter, whom I had known as a three-year-old, gave me a glass of sweet black coffee and a big yellow banana. We sat on the old cane chairs on the verandah, smiling at each other and laughing at all the romping children, and waited for Apit.

When he came, he was dressed in starched khaki clothes (he had been a village elder, now retired, but kept his official uniform for special occasions) and a black *kupia* (cap). His eyes never for a moment left my face as he walked up the path. He still had the same crooked smile and he looked surprisingly youthful. As we clasped each other's hands and looked at each other, the tears ran down our cheeks. Over and over again he repeated *'Njonja Manis'*, *'Njonja Manis'*. Then he asked: 'Your husband?' and I answered: 'He passed away last year,' and he covered his eyes with his hand to show his grief. And then he asked: 'How is Johnny, how is Manya, Peter,

171

Nelleke?' It moved me deeply that this man, who had known us only for about six months thirty years ago, could still remember all the children's names.

I showed him the photos I had with me and gave him a few. He thought that I was a very lucky woman to have had such a large family and I quite agreed with him. Then I told him that I had heard that Atik and Tjètjè had died and he was shocked: 'No, no, not Tjètjè, he is alive and well and lives in Bogor, but yes, Atik died a few years ago.'

'In Bogor?' I asked. 'Can't we go to him? Do you know where he lives?' 'Certainly,' he said. 'We have first coffee together and then I will go with you by bus to Bogor.' Bogor was about an hour's drive from Sukabumi, so I knew I would be able to go there and still be back in Bandung that night. But first I wanted him to have the money, and I was trying to think of a way to give it to him without causing offence. As I gave him the envelope, I said: 'Please, will you organise a big feast for your family to celebrate this happy reunion?' 'Of course,' he said and gave all the money to his first wife, telling her: 'You look after everything.' And I knew that besides the party there would be enough cash for several weeks' food and some new clothes.

I said goodbye to his first wife, her daughter, the older son and the children, and Apit and I took a *bemo* down to Sukabumi,

172

where we found a bus to take us to Bogor and Tjètjè.

CHAPTER SIXTEEN

The bus was old and very noisy and it was drizzling outside; the driver took it easy on the road, much to my relief. Apit and I sat together on the hard seat and occasionally we looked at each other and smiled. Now and then he shook his head in disbelief and once he looked out the window to hide his tears. I took his hand and he squeezed mine. We talked very little, partly because the loud engine drowned out our voices but also because our silence conveyed our emotions more than words could ever have done.

At one point the bus suddenly started to rattle, it shook a bit, and then slowed down until it came to a stop. Apparently breakdowns such as this were common and the passengers did not seem to mind as the silence gave them a chance to talk and gossip.

The driver's young help-mate jumped down from his seat and inspected the motor. The driver shouted some technical advice from his high seat, and handed him a few simple tools. Miraculously the engine responded, first with a few tentative hiccups, then louder, until it was roaring once again.

173

In Bogor Apit called a *bedjak*, a three-wheeled bicycle, like a rickshaw, and we rode through tree-lined streets. 'Here we have to go down,' Apit said, dismissing the *bedjak* driver. 'Give me your umbrella. I hold it for you.' We stood on the side of the road and looked down a path covered with river stones; and large stones, rather like small boulders, lined the path on both sides.

At that moment the sun was just about to set and an orange-purple light was reflected off the wet, glossy stones. Looking up, I saw the large bamboo stand on the right. This was the vision I had the night before, reproduced in minutest detail. What had happened during the night? Why was I given a look at what would take place the next day? Was it to show me that life was not a series of haphazard events, but that it was unfolding according to an ordered plan? It certainly heightened the sense of guidance which I had experienced all along.

'*Njonja,*' Apit's voice brought me back to reality, 'come, we have to go down this path. It leads to the river where Tjètjè's house is. Walk carefully.' He held the umbrella high above my head and together we walked down the rather slippery path, lined on both sides by small houses where the oil lamps had already been lit. People came out and looked with curiosity at the white woman entering their world. It must have looked like a scene from an opera,

with me walking daintily, careful not to slip, and Apit holding the umbrella as if accompanying royalty. I heard him say proudly: 'See this? This is my *Njonja*, she came all the way from the other side of the world, from Australia, especially to visit me.' And I smiled and bowed my head in acknowledgment of their giggles and greetings.

Apit stopped halfway down and I heard him talking to some people. Abruptly he turned to me and looked crestfallen. His voice faltered when he said: '*Njonja*, this is terrible what I just heard. Tjètjè died last week.' Resolutely he grabbed my hand and helped me down the last difficult part of the path. We heard the thundering of the river in the pitch blackness as Apit knocked on the door of the humble bamboo house.

The door was opened into a room crowded with people, mostly women and children. Apit approached respectfully the obvious head of the family, Tjètjè's widow. She was a heavy woman with an impressive face and I was pleased that I recognised her. I took her hand and expressed my sorrow at the loss of her remarkable husband. On the wall hung a recent portrait of Tjètjè, and from a drawer she retrieved a small copy of that photo and gave it to me. He had been sick for a few days and was gone before they realised that his time had come.

We sat and talked, and I reminisced about his special qualities—his loyalty and his sense of humour. She and her daughters and grandchildren were very impressed that their 'Njonja Manis' had travelled so far to try to find him after all those years. As I looked around me at the smiling faces, the lamplight reflecting from their dark eyes and flashing teeth, I felt a very warm, welcome feeling. Realising that here were many hungry mouths to be fed, I gave Tjètjè's widow double the amount I had handed over to Apit. These women would now be able to afford a new sarong for the festivities after the Ramadhan, and there would be plenty of food for some weeks to come. After we said goodbye, the family crowded in front of the house and waved as Apit and I negotiated our way back up the slippery path to the road.

Apit was quiet, deep in his own thoughts, and I knew that he had seen that I had given Tjètjè's widow double the amount of money. I also knew that he expected me to be fair to him and his family, and I racked my brains for a way to offer him a like share, once more without offending him. Suddenly he stopped near a gas lamp-post halfway up the path and asked me: 'What is the time, *Njonja*?' By the light of the lamp I looked at my wristwatch and answered: 'Quarter to seven, Apit.' 'Oh, thank you,' he said, 'I had to ask you as I don't possess a watch myself.' 'Ah,' I said, 'you know what? I am going to give you some extra money so that you can buy yourself a watch. You really need one.' And I gave him the exact amount that would bring his share up to the level of Tjètjè's family.

'Thank you so much, *Njonja*,' he said. 'I am going to buy a watch and I will have engraved in it today's date and the words, *Ini hari, hari untung.*' This meant: Today is a lucky day.

We were both satisfied now and when we sat down on the seat of a waiting *bedjak*, I gave him an envelope for Atik's widow, who now lived in Jakarta. I showed him that the same amount of money was sealed in there. He promised me he would go as soon as possible to Atik's widow in Jakarta (I gave him money for the fare) and convey the many words of appreciation with which I had expressed my admiration and gratitude for what Atik had done for me.

When we reached the market square Apit took me to the bus which went to Bandung. But when it came time for us to say Goodbye, he said to me: 'I am going with you as far as I can, I can take a bus from Tjandjur to Sukabumi. That is not so much longer.' I knew that was not true, but I understood his reluctance to shake hands for the last time.

Once again we were seated on the hard plastic cushions of an old, rattling vehicle which took us through the dark night on the winding mountain roads to Tjandjur, where many passengers had to change buses. Apit and I shook hands, and said to each other: *'Selamat Djalan.'* Bon voyage—what more was there to say? He disappeared quickly into the darkness. The last hour or so gave me plenty of time to reflect on the amazing events of the day. It still felt like a dream and every time my thoughts came back to that incredible moment when I heard Apit's son announcing from the back of the *bemo* that his father had not moved to Jakarta and that he was going to take me to him. The chance of that happening was infinitely remote and yet, it happened! There was no explanation for it. I could only

178

accept, gratefully and humbly, that another miracle had occurred.

By the time I arrived in Bandung at the large bus terminal it was about ten o'clock. Nearby was a waiting area for *bedjaks*, so I sat down in one and asked the driver to take me to the railway station. From there I knew I could catch a taxi or a bus to where my hosts lived. We set off in the *bedjak* and I noticed how quiet the city was, how different from Jakarta. Most people seemed to have gone to bed by that hour, there were not many lights on and the streetlamps were few and far between.

I felt a little bit uneasy and thought I must have looked an easy target, when the driver suddenly left the main street and turned into a very dark, narrow lane. Panic gripped me. 'Detour, *Njonja*,' came the driver's laconic voice. And indeed, when my eyes got used to the darkness, I could see in front of me, here and there, the shapes of other *bedjak* drivers bobbing up and down, working hard to keep their pedals moving.

I sighed with relief and after about ten minutes we joined the main street again. Once more I got a shock. The young fellow stopped his *bedjak* abruptly and came swiftly around and stood in front of me. What will he do to me now? I thought, but I had not much time to panic, as with great care he started fastening a plastic cover which would protect me against the rain which had started to come down again. He made all sorts of reassuring noises, while he checked that the sheet was secure, then he hopped on his bike again and pedalled on to the railway square.

When we arrived there it was raining heavily and there were no taxis in sight. The driver insisted that I remain safe and dry in the *bedjak* until the bus arrived. When it did he helped me up the high step and waved to me as he rode away into the darkness, a slight figure in the soaking rain.

The bus stopped quite near the house, but I still had to wade ankle-deep through water, before I reached the front steps. My friends had been waiting up for me, anxious for my safety. 'Look how bedraggled you are,' they said with concern. 'You must be so tired, what a long day you must have had. But how happy you look!' Dropping my umbrella and kicking off my wet shoes, I smiled at them and said: 'I've had the most wonderful day of my life.'